I0143058

Digging Dusky Diamonds

A History of the
Pennsylvania Coal Region

JOHN R. LINDERMUTH

Digging Dusky Diamonds

Copyright © 2013 by John R. Lindermuth
Cover copyright © 2013 by Sunbury Press, Inc.

All rights reserved, including the right to reproduce this book or
portions thereof in any form whatsoever. For information contact
Sunbury Press, Inc., Subsidiary Rights Dept., 50-A W. Main St.,
Mechanicsburg, PA 17011 USA or legal@sunburypress.com.

For information about special discounts for bulk purchases, please
contact Sunbury Press, Inc. Wholesale Dept. at (855) 338-8359 or
orders@sunburypress.com.

To request one of our authors for speaking engagements or book
signings, please contact Sunbury Press, Inc. Publicity Dept. at
publicity@sunburypress.com.

FIRST SUNBURY PRESS EDITION
Printed in the United States of America
September 2013

Trade paperback ISBN: 978-1-62006-268-5
Mobipocket format (Kindle) ISBN: 978-1-62006-269-2
ePub format (Nook) ISBN: 978-1-62006-270-8

Published by:
Sunbury Press
Mechanicsburg, PA
www.sunburypress.com

SUNBURY
PRESS

Mechanicsburg, Pennsylvania   USA

DEDICATION

For my coal-mining ancestors

Down in a coal mine, underneath the ground,
Where a gleam of sunshine never can be found;
Digging dusky diamonds all the year around,
Away down in a coal mine, underneath the ground.

—Chorus to *Down in a Coal Mine*, Archive of
American Folk Song, Library of Congress

Prologue

The lure of easy fortune is a magnet few can resist. When word of the riches awaiting exploitation in Pennsylvania's anthracite coal region spread in the 1830s it sparked a migration akin to that later recorded for the 1849 California gold rush.

There can be no comparison in terms of numbers, but the situation was similar. Speculators, conmen, and droves of honest men in search of work flocked north from Philadelphia. As one contemporary put it, "the news provoked a frenzy in the city."

"Rumors of fortunes made at a blow, and competency secured by a turn of the fingers, came whispering down the Schuylkill and penetrating the city. Young and old were smitten by the desire to march upon the new Peru, rout the aborigines and sate themselves with wealth," said Joseph Neal.[1]

The dream of easy wealth fizzled when the speculators discovered the best tracts already in the hands of entrepreneurs who had arrived earlier from Sunbury, Pottsville, and Lancaster and Lycoming counties. However, those who came to work found opportunity.

Before 1838, mining in the commonwealth's anthracite coal region was the work of amateurs. Those who owned the land and hoped to profit from it soon saw the need for experienced miners.

English, Welsh, and Scotch-Irish miners who had learned their skills in the old country found ready employment. Irish immigrants who had not worked at mining before found a wide selection of unskilled jobs available, both above and below ground. They sent word home about the opportunities and their number greatly increased during the Potato Famine of the 1840s. By the second generation, many of these Irish were working as

---

1 The Pictorial Sketch-Book of Pennsylvania and its Scenery, Internal Improvements, Resources and Agriculture, Eli Bowen, 1852.

miners. Many Germans also worked in the mines but more worked at carpentry, in trade, as blacksmiths, on the canal boats, and, later, in railroading.

How these people lived and worked, loved and died is recorded in the pages of old newspapers, many of which have been saved to microfilm and are available for scrutiny in historical societies and libraries across the region.

Just as today's newspapers are a reflection of the society reading them, so are these old publications. They reveal the daily concerns—local, national, and international—of the people, their diversions, social attitudes, and prejudices. It's surprising what they disclose that was different about people then and what has remained constant since time immemorial.

We take newspapers for granted today as a primary source of information, but there was a time not so very long ago when they were the main source.

As literacy increased in the United States, newspapers changed from being mainly political organs to the most important sources of information in the nation. They were cheap and readily available almost everywhere. While there were 200 or less newspapers in the country in 1800, the number increased to more than 1,200 by the early 1840s and doubled again by the end of the decade.

Small, hand-run presses made it possible for every town and village to boast its own newspaper and innovation such as the invention of the telegraph in 1844 made for speedy transfer of information from point to point.

What follows is a compilation of the kinds of information available to area newspaper readers in Northumberland and Schuylkill counties, Pennsylvania, in the 19th and early 20th centuries. I hope it will give modern readers an insight into the life of our ancestors in the region.

THE GROWTH OF AN INDUSTRY
1.
Discovery

Bituminous or "soft" coal mining began in the 12th century in Great Britain and by the 16th century it was a familiar household fuel across Europe, so it was not an unknown resource to the American colonists. Soft coal mined in Virginia as early as 1750 helped forge cannonballs for the Revolutionary War.

Coincidentally, anthracite or "hard" coal, which is more difficult to ignite, was first discovered and put to practical use almost simultaneously by three men in three different locations in Pennsylvania. Necho (Nicholas) Allen discovered coal while hunting in 1790 near Pottsville, Schuylkill County, and tested its burning qualities. A year later, the professional hunter, Philip Ginter, made his famous find at Mauch Chunk (now Jim Thorpe), Carbon County. Isaac Tomlinson, a Quaker from Berks County, is credited with the discovery of coal at Shamokin, Northumberland County, in 1790.

Allen eventually formed a partnership with Colonel George Shoemaker and they began mining near Pottsville in 1812. In those early days, the use of anthracite coal as fuel was primarily limited to blacksmiths as the public found it difficult to ignite. It was some years of experimentation by enthusiasts before the public was taught how to burn it. Because of the limited market, Allen soon sold his interest to Shoemaker, who persisted in mining and transporting his coal to Philadelphia in search of a larger market.

Shoemaker's efforts in Philadelphia were vigorous and persistent, and they got him in trouble. Some purchasers who were unsuccessful in getting the coal to burn properly denounced him as a swindler. One "victim" procured a warrant for his arrest. Believing discretion the better part of valor, Shoemaker left the city and took a circuitous route home to avoid the officer of the law.

Workmen building canal boats for the Philadelphia and Reading Railroad during the 1870s. The Schuylkill Canal, covering nearly 60 miles, was used to transport anthracite coal from Port Carbon to Philadelphia.. Courtesy Pennsylvania State Archives.

Colonel Shoemaker was finally successful in inducing several large iron works to use anthracite in their furnaces. Still, the prices coal brought in Philadelphia were barely sufficient to pay the costs of mining and transportation.

That changed with completion of the Schuylkill Canal in 1825. The canal extended from Pottsville to Philadelphia, a distance of more than a hundred miles. In the beginning, there were no tow paths for horses or mules and the boats were either poled or hand drawn by men. The journey took ten days one way. According to a variety of historical sources, the first boat load of Schuylkill County coal was pulled by hand to Philadelphia by Peter Ream, John Rudy, and Daniel Byerly. Peter Ream was my third great-grandfather.

Though Tomlinson and others worked the coal at Shamokin, it wasn't until after the arrival of the visionary John C. Boyd in 1826 that the industry expanded. It would flourish even more in the coming decade with the advent of

4

railroading, when commerce flourished beyond what had been envisioned with development of the canal system.

First Settlers

The first settlers in the Shamokin area came for reasons other than knowledge of the presence of coal.

The Cherrys, who came first, and those who followed in their wake, were doing as pioneers have always done—searching for "greener" pastures in new places.

The impetus for their journey was the so-called "New Purchase." A land office was opened at Fort Augusta, located at what is now Sunbury, in April 1769. Property could be had anywhere in the vast region of the purchase at terms of five pounds sterling per hundred acres plus one penny per acre per year for quit rent. On its first day of business, the land office processed 2,782 applications. By August, the number of applications had reached 4,000. With such rapid growth, it was deemed necessary to found a new county to govern the settlers.

Northumberland County was established on March 21, 1772, a territory almost one-third the area of the commonwealth. Eventually, twenty-six counties would be carved from this original "mother" county.

This growth of population was only one phase of expansion along the eastern seaboard between 1760-76 as people moved inland to unexplored territories. Hector St. John de Crevecoeur, who was himself among those who emigrated from Connecticut to the Wyoming district of Pennsylvania, voiced amazement at the number of people involved and the risks they were willing to take, noting that the "... settlers scatter themselves here and there in the bosom of such an extensive country without even a previous path to direct their steps and without being in any number sufficient either to protect or assist one another."

Abraham Cherry could have gone in any direction from Sunbury. Perhaps it was only a whim that took him southeast or, maybe, it was a desire for isolation. If it was the latter case, his choice was well made.

Sketch of Fort Augusta near Sunbury, PA. Courtesy of the Northumberland County Historical Society.

The 400-plus acres comprising what is now Shamokin are squeezed in a narrow valley between steep, boulder-strewn mountains. The lowest parts of the valley along the winding creek were then thick swamp bounded by groves of pine, hemlock, and laurel. The town of Sunbury, about twenty miles north, was not laid out until 1772 and the closest real markets for produce would have been Reading or Easton, either a journey of a week or more away.

Despite unpromising circumstance, isolation, privation, danger from American Indian attack and natural calamity, the Cherrys dug in and began carving out a home in this unlikely setting. That they and their neighbors persevered illustrates a remarkable strength of character and determination.

Although Abraham Cherry was the first settler, the bulk of the land in Shamokin proper was contained in three tracts all acquired by speculators in 1773. These were the William Tomlinson, or "Stonehenge," on which coal was first discovered and put to practical use; the Samuel Clark, which was subsequently purchased at sheriff sale by Jesse Major; and the Samuel Wetherill.

While coal was not Cherry's objective in coming to the territory, he could not have been oblivious to its presence.

6

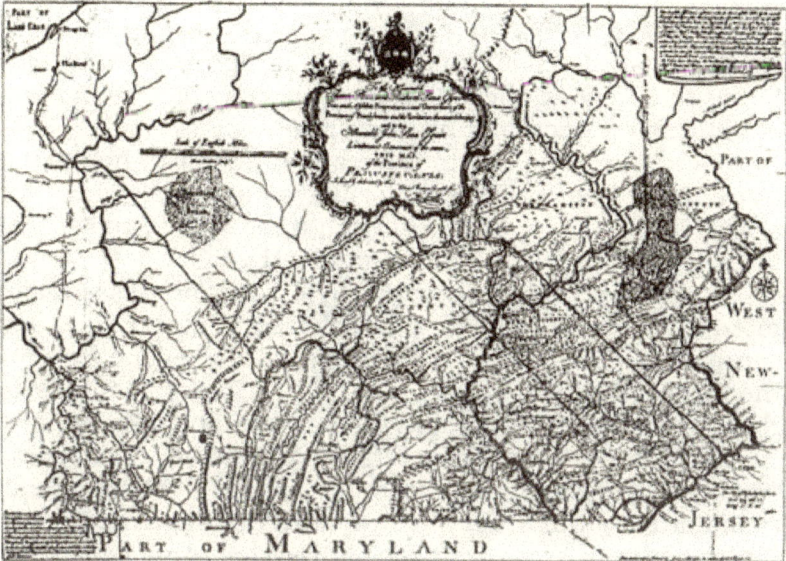

Map of Pennsylvania by William Scull 1770. Courtesy of the National Park Service.

He would have seen it in outcroppings where seams were exposed by the action of water or as "smut" or "blossom" (decomposition in the soil). That the American Indians were familiar with this mineral is also a certainty. There are records of their having used it in trade as early as 1750, and in 1766 a party of Nanticoke, Conoy, and Mohicans visited the governor at Philadelphia and complained of white men robbing their mine in the Wyoming area.

The existence of coal is noted on the Scull Map, printed and issued at Philadelphia on April 4, 1770. Several of the designated sites are in Schuylkill County near Minersville and Ashland. The mineral may have been pointed out to traders and surveyors by the American Indians, though its usefulness was still unsuspected.

Written accounts reveal that Cherry exhibited specimens to visitors as curiosities. As a farmer and sawyer, Cherry underestimated the value of this resource.

7

The Coming of Jesse

While some might take a peculiar pride in having a horse thief among their ancestors there's some reluctance about linking a community's origin to a scalawag.

There's been no call to raise a monument in his honor, but a rogue named Jesse Major played a pivotal role in the origin of Shamokin. For those with a taste for a bit of color in their history, Major more than fills the bill.

Though he worked occasionally as a tailor, Jesse Major more often made his living as a horse thief, burglar, and counterfeiter and had a reputation so sullied he became the prime suspect in virtually any crime committed in Northumberland County and the surrounding area.

Jesse is described in several county histories as being "very fleet of foot," though it is not certain if this is related to his attempts to evade the law or to the wagering on foot races that were a common social diversion in those pioneer days at the beginning of the 19th century. Perhaps both apply since he was a known gambler as well as a criminal.

Now, if Jesse had an arch enemy it had to be Sheriff Walter Brady, who relentlessly tracked him down and put him behind bars on more than one occasion.

Though he served as sheriff from 1815-1818, Brady apparently was not above a little gambling of his own. Sometime around 1819, Sheriff Brady came into possession of a tract of land that would be among the valuable real estate in what was to become Shamokin. Unfortunately, his land speculations got ahead of his income and the property was seized by the court and put up for auction.

But, at the time, there was no Shamokin and the tract was raw land in a wilderness. No bidders came forward to relieve the ex-sheriff of his debts. On August 19, 1824, the property came on the block again at the courthouse in Sunbury.

According to the histories, Jesse Major had just been released from another of his frequent visits to the county lockup when he chanced by the auction site and made a bid of $12 for the sheriff's property. Since he was well known around the courthouse and assumed to be destitute after his incarceration, no one took his bid seriously until he stepped forward and paid up in gold. In light of his reputation as a counterfeiter, it is certain some testing of his coin took place before the deed was delivered.

Jesse Major's purchase should not be construed as an attempt to go straight and secure respectability as a landowner. More likely his action was a mocking revenge on Walter Brady for his past persecutions.

Whatever comment Brady may have had has been lost to history. Most likely, with a chuckle gurgling in his throat at Brady's chagrin, landowner Major headed south on foot to explore his realm. What he expected is also lost to history. What he saw must have given him cause to regret his desire for revenge.

Traversing what once had been grandly known as the Great Highway and was now called the Reading Road and was, in fact, a mere dirt track through thick forest, "so entangled with brambles even the rabbits cannot penetrate," according to one chronicle, Jesse came at length, after a long, hot, dusty walk, to a tavern at Snufftown (now Paxinos), the last outpost of civilization.

Here he learned more wilderness lay ahead. Though the American Indians were long gone and he had no money to tempt any lurking highwaymen, it was certain his tracks would be dogged by panthers, wolves, and bears, and he would have to tread carefully to avoid the timber rattlers and copperheads that abounded on sunlit patches along the trail. It can be assumed that he who never before bought a horse might have wished he had instead of buying this pig in a poke. Still, he had come this far and he might as well go on.

Finally, he reached his destination and found that the only inhabitants were a family named Cherry; one Solomon Dunkelberger; Benjamin Campbell, whose property adjoined Jesse's; and the widow of William Ducher, who recently had been murdered by unknown persons. A few solitary hunters ranged the hills. Martin and George Goss grazed a few cattle and fattened hogs among the marshes in what would later become the nearby village of Tharptown and farmed on the surrounding hills.

If these isolated settlers were glad to see another human being, their destitute condition hardly raised the optimism of a man who hoped to profit from his speculation (the glorious taste of revenge surely having abated).

The Cherry brothers had abandoned hope of raising enough from the stony soil to support their families. Their father, Abraham, had raised a rudimentary sawmill on the perky creek that rushed around the seven hills and flowed north to join the Susquehanna from whence Jesse had come. One of the brothers had started a distillery on another hillside. Despite their enterprise, there was no market for the lumber or liquor and they remained as poor as before. Perhaps they were more optimistic about the future than Jesse. It seemed no one had found a profitable use for the land since it had been surveyed by Samuel Clark in 1776.

While they talked, one of the settlers showed the new landowner some unusual rocks his boys had found along the creek bank. Black they were, and different from other stones Jesse had seen before, and they intrigued him. There was something about these rocks that sparked a chord in his memory. Jesse kept his counsel and mulled on it and that night as he lay awake in his bed it came to him. A man named Tomlinson had found similar rocks here years earlier. Coal, he had called it, and proclaimed it as the fuel for the future. Jesse wasn't certain but he thought Tomlinson had profited from coal and so, he thought, might he.

Secretly, the next day, Jesse Major gathered more of the rocks from along the creek, stored them in his pack sack, and headed back to civilization to seek his fortune. At Paxinos, he induced a blacksmith to try some coal on his forge. But the fuel exploded on the hearth and the smithy pronounced it worthless.

Crisscrossing the country, Jesse visited every wealthy man he could. Unfortunately his unsavory reputation preceded him, and none chose to invest. It was nearly two years before his luck changed.

Worn out and impecunious in his trial honesty, Jesse Major stopped one evening in the spring of 1826 at Joseph

Snyder's tavern, the Liberty Pole, near Paxinos. Desperate, he offered to trade his tract for a horse. Snyder declined but suggested Jesse see a man he knew who was fond of speculation.

John C. Boyd was indeed a man who loved speculation, and it had made him wealthy. He lived in a manor house by the Susquehanna near Danville, reaping coin from a grist mill, a thousand acres of farmland, and shrewd investments in the enterprises of others.

Boyd proved ripe for another speculation—one that would increase his wealth and take it away several times over. After inspecting Jesse's property, Boyd purchased the tract of 160 acres and 80 perches on May 1, 1826, for $230 and an old gray mare valued at fifty dollars.

Successful at last as an honest man, Jesse Major mounted the mare and rode off into legend.

The rest is history.

The Enterprising Boyd

Had he not been a speculator, Boyd might have been inclined to regret his purchase of this property when first he gazed upon it.

It would not have been an encouraging site to a lesser man. His tract was part of some 400 acres comprising a narrow valley constricted between rugged mountains—a landscape indeed that possessed little incentive even to the Indians as permanent settlers. The lower portion of the tract was a thickly wooded swamp bisected by a winding creek and, on the higher elevations, the land was stony and thin-soiled.

But Boyd was no ordinary man, nor was he the type to buy a proverbial pig in a poke.

Born in Chester County and one of eight children of a Revolutionary War general, Boyd came to what is now Montour County in 1820, married the daughter of another general, Daniel Montgomery, the founder of Danville, and commenced operation of a store. From that point his career was upwardly mobile. From the store he expanded to vast land holdings and a grist mill conveniently located along the Susquehanna River.

When he came to inspect the tract at Shamokin he was already cognizant of the potential value of coal and involved in other enterprises that would help him exploit it.

Undoubtedly, a man as astute as Boyd was aware of earlier coal discoveries and efforts to profit from them.

As early as 1762, settlers from Connecticut reported discoveries of coal in Pennsylvania's Wyoming Valley. Differing from the soft bituminous English coal they may have been familiar with, they referred to it as "stone coal." Charles Stewart noted "stone coal" locations on the map for his survey of lands opposite present day Wilkes-Barre in 1768. Specimens of this coal were sent to Britain for experimentation, but repeated trials failed to find a way to make it burn.

Godcharles[2] contends stone coal was used by the garrison at Fort Augusta, quoting Colonel William Plunket, who was among those who built the fort at Sunbury in 1756. This is borne out by records of the British War Office.

Again according to Godcharles, an Ensign Holler who was part of the garrison in 1758, reported quarters were heated that winter with stone coal, some of which was brought downriver from near Nanticoke and also a wagon load acquired some six leagues from the fort (in the vicinity of Shamokin-Mount Carmel).

Obadiah Gore, a blacksmith, is credited as the first to achieve a means of igniting and burning anthracite coal in his forge. The success of his experiments became known and use of anthracite as a fuel spread to other forges and furnaces in the Wyoming Valley. The first coal ever shipped from that valley was sent by the proprietary government of Pennsylvania to an armory at Carlisle to be used in the production of firearms for the Continental army.

Because of the difficulties of transportation and combustion, anthracite was not widely used outside the valley for some time though there were a number of significant discoveries elsewhere in what would become known as the Eastern, Western Middle, and Southern coal fields.

---

2   Daily Stories of Pennsylvania, Frederic A. Godcharles, Milton PA
     1924.

As previously noted, Isaac Tomlinson, a Quaker from Berks County, made the earlier discovery at Shamokin. His father, William Tomlinson, owned a tract called "Stonehenge," adjoining that purchased by Boyd and which he had leased to the elder Cherry. William Tomlinson never moved to Shamokin. Young Isaac was often sent by his father on inspection tours of this property.

On one of these inspection tours in 1790 Isaac Tomlinson found a vein of coal exposed by the rushing waters of Quaker Run, a stream named for the property owner's religious affiliation. He took samples of the ore back to Berks County and tried them on his father's forge.

Those experiments raised exciting prospects. Tomlinson saw his coal as a substitute for Virginia bituminous. The anthracite found elsewhere in the commonwealth was difficult to ignite. This was softer, burned easier, and had properties similar to that with which people were familiar.

Confident that there was potential in the fuel, Tomlinson moved to Stonehenge around 1795 and opened an inn. He also built a blacksmith shop that was operated by his brother, Thomas, and which was fueled entirely with coal from their Quaker Run mine. Tomlinson was, thus, the first person to discover Shamokin coal and his smithy was the only one at that time outside the Wyoming Valley to use "stone coal" as fuel.

Other Ventures

It would be a great stretch of the imagination to say Tomlinson "profited" from his mine and even more to say it made him wealthy. Though he may have seen potential for the use of coal as fuel, his heart was obviously in farming and his experiments with coal were no more than a curious toying with an interesting substance.

When rediscovered more than a century later, his original mine was found to be no more than a small quarry from which sufficient coal for his experiments was mined. There is no evidence he attempted to market it or otherwise make broader use of his discovery.

Tomlinson's quarry was located in December 1897 by Dr. J. J. John, Edward Brennan, a mine inspector, and

Patrick Brennan. It was located on the north bank of Quaker Run, about 900 feet west of what was then known as the Scott shaft.

From this small quarry it is reported that a 15-year-old youth named John Thompson dug a two-horse load of coal in 1815. Thompson hauled his coal to Sunbury where he sold it for $5 to a shoemaker who used it to heat his home. This was the first Shamokin coal that went to market.

There was another discovery of coal in the area after Tomlinson's find that applies to our story.

Farmers fording Shamokin Creek noticed shiny black stones in the water. Curious as to their origin, they proceeded upstream until they found a seam of coal that had been exposed by the flow of water. This was a vein of free-burning red-ash coal similar to that found at Stonehenge.

Over time, quantities of this coal were quarried and its burning qualities were tested with varying success.

To say coal was mined at this time is to misstate the situation; quarrying would be a better term. The first coal mined in this region was simply retrieved from the stream bed or dug up where the veins were exposed by the action of water. It would be some time before actual mining was undertaken.

This particular quarry begun by those farmers was on land owned by Jacob and Mary Tomlinson, grandchildren of William Tomlinson, and it was part of the Samuel Clark survey. Eventually, the tract would be sold by the county commissioners for back taxes. The purchaser was Sheriff Walter Brady.

As we already know, Brady was in debt when he left office. His bondsmen had this tract put up at sheriff's sale and it was purchased by Jesse Major who, in turn, sold it to John Boyd.

The history of that momentous transaction is recorded in county records:

James R. Shannon, Sheriff, Northumberland County, to Jesse Major, deed dated Aug. 20, 1824, consideration $12 for all interest in Samuel Clark survey belonging to

Walter Brady, entered March 1, 1826, Deed Book V, Page 667.

Jesse Major and wife to John C. Boyd and John Housel, deed dated May 1, 1826, consideration $230 for Brady interest previously mentioned, entered June 25, 1826, Deed Book W, Page 38.

John M. Housel and wife to John C. Boyd, assignment dated June 15, 1826, consideration $100, for all interest in Brady tract.

Housel must have considered himself a shrewd speculator. He had bought Jacob Tomlinson's portion of the Clark survey for $5 on May 12, 1826, which he also sold to Boyd on June 15 for $100.

Boyd's first venture in mining on his new property was described by Joseph Bird, a participant in the project:

> In 1826, John C. Boyd and my father, Ziba Bird, built a dam in Shamokin creek north of Webster street and opened a coal mine. The coal was mined out of the bottom of the creek. The vein had been discovered some years before, being exposed by the action of the water. My father was the miner and John Runkle wheeled the coal to the bank on a plank, assisted by myself, who was then a small boy. Casper Reed and Samuel Startzel were hired to haul this coal from Shamokin to Boyd's place, two miles above Danville. They were several months at the job. The coal was then put in arks and floated down the river to Columbia. This was the first Shamokin coal that was mined and sent to market.[3]

Bird evidently was unaware of Thompson's earlier mining and marketing operation.

Boyd's initial venture in mining did not immediately lead to the founding of a community. His operation proved the potential existed for sale of the product. But, it was a cumbersome project and hardly profitable. As Bird describes above, the coal was mined, then transported to Boyd's farm along the river where it was loaded on the arks

---

3   History of Northumberland County, Pa., edited by Herbert C. Bell, Chicago, 1891.

and taken down to Columbia and there offered for sale. The condition of roads at the time, the whims of weather and the river, and the difficulty of convincing people of the merits of coal, all consumed man hours and subtracted from possible profit.

Perhaps a single-minded entrepreneur could have made a go of it. Boyd's far-flung interests detracted from his mining enterprise. He continued to speculate.

One of the enterprises that attracted his attention at that time was the manufacture of iron. Henry Myers had purchased Solomon Dunkelberger's holdings on the west side of the Gap and commenced to build a charcoal furnace. The furnace operated with bog ore found in the vicinity of Furnace Run and charcoal made at the site. Boyd invested in the project and, according to some accounts, suffered "serious financial loss" when it failed. A lack of sufficient limestone was apparently a major factor in the failure of the furnace.

Presumably because of the financial losses he had suffered, Boyd sold some of his coal lands to Jacob Graeff, who made the first attempt at founding a town on the site.

The Naming of a Town

Though John C. Boyd acquired the tract we now know as Shamokin in 1826 from Jesse Major, horse thief and counterfeiter, the community wasn't known by its present name until 1840.

Boyd's initial interest being in speculation and profit from known coal deposits, he sold part of the original tract to Jacob Graeff of Reading. Graeff took the first steps toward developing a town, surveying a portion of his land, clearing some brush, and laying out a street in 1830. His work attracted little attention from potential settlers.

Construction on the Danville and Pottsville Railroad between Sunbury and Locust Gap in 1834 inspired town-building on the part of Boyd. He proposed to call his town Marion, until discovering the name already had been taken by another community.

His second choice was Shamokin, derived from the American Indian name for the council village located at the

1864 map of Shamokin, P.A.

present site of Sunbury. This name also had other usages in the county, though not for a community. It had been applied variously to the creek that still flows through Shamokin and up to the Susquehanna at Sunbury, to a large township (which originally included all of Ralpho and Catawissa townships), and the original post office name for Paxinos.

Shortly after Boyd laid out his town, a syndicate of Sunbury residents acquired Graeff's title and developed another town they called Groveville. The name of this town honored the maiden name of Mrs. William McCarty, wife of the head of the Sunbury group.

Neither name—Shamokin or Groveville—proved popular with the first settlers who commonly referred to their places of residence as either "Boydtown" or "Newtown." It wasn't until 1840 that the name Shamokin was applied to the Coal Township Post Office and caught on with the public as the two communities merged into one.

As to the name Shamokin, controversy surrounds its origin and meaning. John Heckewelder, a Moravian missionary to the American Indians, thought it came from mispronunciation of a Delaware (Lenni-Lenape) phrase meaning "where we fished for eels." Abraham L. Guss, another early writer on the Indians of Pennsylvania, claims it meant "where the chief lives," while Dr. George P. Donehoo's "place of the horns" can be seen on the state historical commission sign at the city boundaries.

The village site on the Susquehanna predates both the Delaware and their conquerors, the Iroquois. It's probable that the Susquehannocks occupied the site as early as the 15th century. Sassoonan, head chief of the Unami Delaware, moved to Shamokin circa 1718. Shikellamy was sent by the Iroquois Confederacy in 1728 to govern subject peoples, which included the Delaware and a large contingent of refugees from other tribes.

Pioneer Life

What was life like for those early pioneers in the coal region towns? An interview in the May 7, 1885 edition of the *Shamokin Herald* with Benjamin McClow provides some insight.

Deer and fish were plentiful in the area. "Coal Run, Shamokin Creek and Carbon Run were noted for trout, and many a deer fell a victim to the unerring aim of the flintlock rifles in the hands of Mr. McClow and Peter Boughner."

Born June 25, 1812, near Elysburg, McClow came with his family to Shamokin in 1838 when there were only three houses in the town. He erected a house at what is now the corner of Commerce and Pearl but was then in the midst of thick forest.

McClow engaged in operating a sawmill—the second in the community. He told the *Herald* reporter that demand for board was so great in the developing town he was compelled to work day and night.

He said his grandfather (it isn't clear whether he meant Cornelius McClow or his maternal grandfather, Benjamin Campbell) discovered coal while digging a mill race below the Cameron breaker site and it was taken to Elysburg on sleds during the winter for use of blacksmiths.

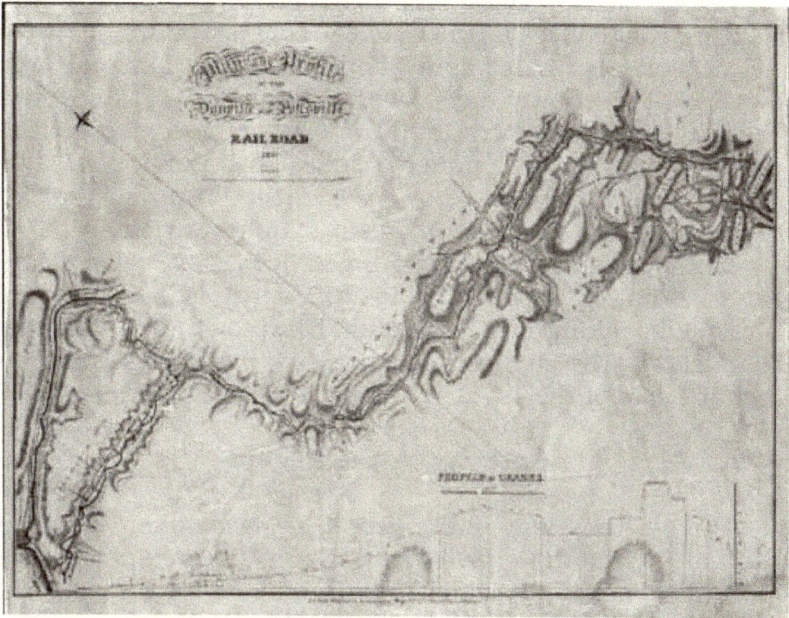

A map of the 1831 plan, and a profile of the elevations, for the construction of the Danville-Pottsville Railroad. Courtesy of Library of Congress, Geography and Map Division.

McClow also commented on the coming of the railroad:

Two small locomotives were put on the track and when they departed from town some of the visitors from the Mahanoy valley ran after them to catch them but were not successful. The engines being too heavy for the tracks they were abandoned until heavier rails were laid, and horses were used to take the coal over the road to the canal at Sunbury.

The pioneer said during the winter when the canal was frozen that work was scarce and properties were sold cheap. He added that money was scarce at all times. Coal operators settled with their employees once a year and payment was principally in store goods. "Flour could be bought cheaper at Pottsville and sent to Shamokin by farmers passing between the two places. The sight of a silver dollar in cash was good for sore eyes to a working man in those days."

Later, McClow was employed grading railroads and erecting coal chutes for the pioneer coal operators.

McClow also noted that John Boyd, the principal land owner in those early days, offered to give a lot to the first bride in Shamokin. Mr. and Mrs. Joseph Bird received the deed for that lot on Commerce, just above Pearl. Boyd also offered a lot for the first boy born in the town and that lot at Sunbury and Pearl streets went to John Snyder.

McClow showed the reporter a deed that belonged to his grandfather giving title to 700 acres of land west of Shamokin, taking in Scotch Hill, Tharptown, and valuable coal tracts. He commented that his mother planted an orchard east of the Trout Run dam at Tharptown.

Gateway to the Region

Though they may share little else in common with the Eternal City, both Pottsville and Shamokin are spread (like ancient Rome) over a series of hills.

John Pott Jr., a Berks County native and entrepreneur, acquired the site of this community in 1808 and laid out the plot for the town named for him in 1816. Of course there were people living in the area much earlier. There is the tradition of the Neiman family being massacred by American Indians during the Revolutionary War near the present site of the Pottsville Hospital.

Pott bought the tract from Lewis Reese, Isaac Thomas, and the widow of Lewis Morris, three men who had earlier plans of profiting from a site few of their contemporaries envisioned as the nucleus for a prosperous city. My fourth great-grand uncle, John Reed, had been hired by this trio as superintendent of a crew building a dam and laying the foundation for an iron furnace and forge. John's son, Jeremiah, born December 19, 1800, is believed to be the first white child born in what is now the city. Jeremiah became a coal merchant and was sheriff of Schuylkill County from 1843-46. Pott's daughter, Hannah, was the first white girl born in the community.

There were more than 500 homes in the town and numerous mercantile establishments by 1831. Pottsville became the county seat in 1851. Pott, his sons, and

View of Pottsville, Pennsylvania; an engraving published October 1854 in Gleason's Pictorial Drawing Room Companion, Boston, Massachusetts. Courtesy of Wikipedia.

other speculators expanded on the original boundaries of the town over a period of years.

Considered by many as the gateway to the anthracite coal region, Pottsville has profited over the years from the mining of that resource—from railroading, beer, textiles, and other industries—far beyond the imagination of those who scoffed at those early visionaries. There is some evidence coal was mined within the city limits as early as 1784 and the drift opened by Benjamin Pott in 1824 may have been on this same site.

The Yuengling Brewery (now both the oldest and the largest family-owned in the US), the novels of John O'Hara, and an expanding tourist interest in coal region history continue to help spread the fame of Pottsville to other regions.

Glowing Predictions

It's common practice today for communities to advertise in an attempt to attract industry. In the early days of

21

anthracite mining, promoters advertised in hope of attracting settlers and investors to build a community around the industry.

They often did this in the form of letters to newspapers, which were sometimes copied by other publications.

An example of this is a letter found in the June 23, 1838 edition of the *Sunbury Gazette* and *Miner's Register*. This letter from an unidentified promoter had appeared previously in the *Lycoming Gazette* and *Chronicle*. It offers an interesting perspective on Shamokin at that time and what entrepreneurs hoped it might become. It reads, in part:

> The town of SHAMOKIN is situated 19 miles from Sunbury and about 13 from Danville, on the Danville, Sunbury and Pottsville railroad, which is completed from Sunbury one mile and a half beyond it. The advantages the town possesses are that it is in the midst of one of the finest fields of Anthracite coal in the Union—that it has already a means of communication with the river, by which almost any quantity of coal can be sent to market—that its location is good in regard to the procuring of the necessaries of life—that it is healthy—the water pure, and that there is abundant space to build.

The writer noted that the town contained about 30 or 40 well-built houses and he speculated another 20 would be put up in that year. He also contended that a locomotive would run to the river at Sunbury at least twice a day within a month or so.

He predicted that those who purchased land would see its value double in less than five years.

The editor of the newspaper saw fit to add (for which he may have been compensated):

> There is no part of Pennsylvania that offers a more favorable opportunity for a profitable investment than this region. Coal land can now be purchased at a very reasonable price, and as the improvements for bringing down the Coal to Sunbury, immediately upon the great

basin formed by the Shamokin dam, are about being completed, they will soon be greatly enhanced in value. This region possesses superior advantages. The mountains are generally high, there is a vast body of coal above the water level, the veins are numerous and large, varying from five to 70 feet in thickness, and the coal [is] inferior in quality to none, and for manufacturing purposes it has been tried and pronounced superior to any anthracite now in use.

Canal Complaints

Just two years after the completion of the Erie Canal in New York, Pennsylvania commenced building a canal in 1827 from the Juniata River and along the west bank of the Susquehanna River to Northumberland and then on to Wilkes-Barre. A west branch of the canal continued north to Muncy and, eventually, connected to the Erie Canal.

This system made Northumberland an important junction in the days before the canals were supplanted by the railroad. Because of its economic value to the region, one would suppose all were happy with the actions of the canal board. Such was not the case—as was made plain by an editorial in the May 11, 1833 edition of the *Workingmen's Advocate*, published at Sunbury.

"Through ignorance or design," the article lamented, "the canal board of 1827 committed an error, against every demonstration and every remonstrance, by locating the canal on the wrong side of the river below Sunbury."

The editorial contended that the placement of the canal was detrimental to the success of mine operations in the Mahanoy coal fields and that the canal board followed up its error the next year by recommending a railroad from Columbia to Philadelphia in preference to continuation of the canal to the Chesapeake Bay.

"Men took precedence in the management of the canal who were only eminent for scalping panthers, wolves and wild cats," the editorialist thundered.

The county of Northumberland, with the largest body of Anthracite coal in the known world, would ere now have been the receiver and dispenser of immeasurable wealth to this Community, if the canal system had been prosecuted in accordance with the dictates of sound policy.

While Schuylkill, by means of an expenditure less than two million of dollars is receiving from the sea board one million of dollars annually for coal; and while the Mauch Chunk Company have had their operations aided and borne out by the State expenditure, in making 70 miles of canal, the Coal fields of Mahanoy appear as far in the back ground as ever.

Creek Navigation

Though not often thought of as a navigable stream, a canal boat was built on and floated down Shamokin Creek to the Susquehanna and beyond.

Dr. Robert H. Awl of Sunbury recalled the event in a story in the *Sunbury Daily Item*, which was repeated in the *Shamokin Herald* on December 12, 1890. Awl, who was born in 1819, said he believed the canal boat built in 1832 or 1833 was the only one ever constructed and run on the creek.

He said it was built by Adam Shissler, Jacob Martz, and some others on the north side of Shamokin Creek on a farm owned in 1890 by Benjamin Zettlemoyer.

Dr. Awl said:

In the Spring when the creek got high, they launched her in the stream and came down all right to Leisenring's fording (between L. T. Rohrbach's and Charles Rhinehart's farm). Here the boat stuck, but after working and prying a long time, they got off.

She then ran all right until she came to the mill dam. This took one day. In the morning they tried skids to slide her over the dam. This would not work and the boat stuck on the dam.

The men got a jack and attempted to lift the craft. When this also didn't work they got ropes around the boat and a windlass on shore and tried to pull the craft over. But it still wouldn't move.

As they pondered what to do, a heavy storm came up. The rain raised the water and lifted the boat over the dam and sent it sailing down the creek with the crew onboard as hundreds of spectators watched from the shore. Among those on the boat were John Shissler, William Martz, and Aaron Vansickle.

The boat stuck again on an island near a log mill. As the creek was still rising and it was feared the boat wouldn't pass under the bridge at the point, people on shore pulled it off with ropes.

The boat was loaded with flour and when the creek receded enough for it to pass under the bridge, the craft sailed down to Clark's Ferry where it entered the canal. On this, its maiden voyage, the boat went on to Havre de Grace, Philadelphia, and the Schuylkill Canal where it was caught in another freshet, went over a mill dam, and was lost.

Coming of the Railroad

The importance of railroads to the area's early commerce is demonstrated by an article on the opening of the western division of the Pottsville and Danville railroad published in the December 5, 1835 edition of the *Workingmen's Advocate*.

The article also presents a glimpse of the scenery to be seen along the route, including a pristine Shamokin Creek.

The story reports that about 30 persons clambered aboard two new passenger cars built at Pottsville to the "... ringing of bells and the joyful cheers of the traveling party and spectators" at noon in Sunbury.

Nearly the whole of this division of the road is laid through a series of farms, where level meadows and plentiful orchards, the undulating hills on either hand, often cultivated to the summit, and the tall timber of the valley, through which, at intervals, gleams the silver-faced Shamokin Creek, winding its way to the

Susquehanna, form altogether such scenery as is rarely equaled.

The newspaper stressed the economic value of this avenue between the Susquehanna and the Schuylkill.

The Girard coal field, now the estate of Philadelphia, and the Shamokin field, also, abound with anthracite coal of the best quality. The former with the timber of the Mahanoy valley, is now transported by the eastern part of this railroad to the Schuylkill; and five or six hundred tons per day can be passed over the planes; while the contents of the Shamokin mines will be sent westward, to the canal basin at Sunbury. The cars returning from Sunbury, which otherwise would be empty, will convey, eastward, the produce brought down the two branches of the Susquehanna, and those returning from the Schuylkill, will convey westward, merchandise from Philadelphia through the centre of Pennsylvania and to the centre of the state of New York. Thus a rapid and reciprocal trade, of the most advantageous nature, will be prosecuted by a route seventy miles nearer than by the Union canal.

It was also noted that mail would arrive at Sunbury from Philadelphia in a mere 10 hours, or a third of the time previously required.

The Shamokin Valley was a natural choice for the new railroad line, since there were no mountains to obstruct the route and it could be graded at limited expense in a short period of time. The greatest problem was the necessity of erecting six bridges over the Shamokin Creek.

The first locomotive here was the North Star, which drew two passenger cars, the Shamokin and the Mahanoy, and some 30 four-wheeled trucks fitted with seats. Many who took the inaugural ride had never seen a locomotive before and records state women and children were frightened by the shrill whistle and the hiss of escaping steam.

Noting that the locomotive was a wood burner, one account said "The passengers, to protect themselves from the burning sparks, raised their umbrellas and parasols. These were burnt full of holes and many of the people had their clothes ruined."

The Shamokin and the Mahanoy were termed "pleasure cars," each seating about 18 persons. Fare to Sunbury from Shamokin was 50 cents.

A few months later, the Mountaineer, a second locomotive, was added to the fledgling line. Coal tonnage for 1838 was just over 4,000 tons.

By 1844, the Philadelphia & Reading Railroad had been extended to Pottsville. Kimber Cleaver, the Shamokin engineer, surveyed a new route and a charter was obtained for a new line, the Shamokin, Mahanoy, and Schuylkill Railroad Company, which was able to connect with the P&R at Pottsville.

This provided a continuous road of more than 150 miles, allowing the cheap and rapid transit of product all the way from Shamokin to Philadelphia and the seaboard.

Census Facts

The census is among the most valued tools of the genealogist. It is equally important to the historian. You don't have to be either to find it interesting.

For example, let's examine some basic facts from the census of 1840 and how they relate to Northumberland County and its residents of the time. The census for that year showed 1,724,033 residents in Pennsylvania and just over 20,000 in Northumberland County.

In 1840, the number of persons employed in mining in the county was only 53 while 2,758 persons worked at agriculture. Other employment included: commerce, 50; manufacturing and trades, 1,297; navigation of canals, lakes and rivers, 66; and learned professions and engineering, 68. The number of persons at public charge was stated as thirteen.

There were 61 primary and common schools in the county with a total of 2,854 students, 35 of whom were at public charge. The number of persons over the age of 20 who could not read and write was said to be seventy-three.

The *Sunbury American* newspaper took hot exception to that last figure, stating that it must be an error because the number in Union County was given as six.

Twenty persons living in the county were receiving pensions for service in the Revolutionary War. The county had three persons with hearing and speech deficiencies and eight who were blind.

Another interesting fact is that the county had a significant population of free blacks in 1840 including 11 males and 21 females under 10 years; 19 males and 18 females between 10 and 24; 12 males and 9 females between 24 and 36; nine males and three females between 36 and 55; and five males and one female above fifty-five.

The *Sunbury American* commented on June 26, 1841 that: "There are 64 slaves in the state. Slavery was abolished in Pennsylvania in 1780. No person born after that period can be held in involuntary servitude. All the slaves therefore must be over 60 years old, and when they die, slavery will have become extinct in this state."

Big Mountain

The Big Mountain Coal and Improvement Company was one of numerous mine operators in the Shamokin coal region. It began operations in 1853, eventually had four collieries—Buck Ridge, Big Mountain, Henry Clay, and Garfield—and remained active until 1932.

An article in the April 22, 1854 edition of the *Sunbury Gazette* predicted an optimistic outlook for the fledgling company. That article said the firm had 3,000 acres on Buck Run by charter and another 3,000 acres held in trust.

The stock of the company was subscribed in the latter part of March 1853 and, in the ensuing year, the article said the company had been busy opening mines, completing its railroad, and readying the collieries for lease. "The improvements are a large steam saw mill, a railroad from the mines to Shamokin, one and quarter miles long, a coal breaker, capable of preparing 150,000 tons per annum, a colliery, from five gangways, with a capacity of 200,000 tons per annum."

Additionally, it was reported that nine houses were occupied, 10 more were under roof and another 20 were being built.

The article quoted Bettle Paul:

It is worthy of remark that improvements made thus far will cost but about $45,000, whereas in Schuylkill County, $50,000 to $75,000 is required to open a colliery, etc., simply to send out 100,000 tons of coal. Our expenditure has not only established the colliery, but has made the railroad, and put us in a condition to take out not less than 75,000 tons the first year.

Commenting on the means by which the coal would be taken to market, the article referred to the Pennsylvania Canal, which could supply towns all along the Susquehanna and down to Baltimore, and the Coal Run Railroad, which was expected to be completed within a year and would open the New York market coal trade.

The Mine Hill road will soon be done to Ashland, thus leaving but four miles to finish between Philadelphia and our coal region. The Danville road, when completed, and its friends are sanguine of its early accomplishment, will dispose of 200,000 tons per annum. The Susquehanna road which will connect with the Philadelphia and Sunbury railroad at Sunbury, although it has been under a cloud during the winter, must come out eventually triumphant—so positive a commercial necessity as that road is, cannot be avoided; as to the Sunbury and Erie road, the making of it is a settled fact, though its completion is a question of time.

Interesting Statistics

An article in the August 13, 1853 edition of the *Sunbury Gazette* provides some interesting statistics on the state of mining in Schuylkill County at that time.

The report was compiled by C. W. Peale and J. M. Weatherill for the World's Fair to be held at New York.

Early Reading Railroad steam engine -- Reading class A-4b Camelback (0-4-0) #1248, location and date unknown. One example of this type (and the only Reading Camelback) has been preserved at the Railroad Museum of Pennsylvania. (photo: RCT&HS Archives)

According to the article, 9,792 persons were employed, both inside and outside, at the various mines. The mines utilized 468 horses and 569 mules. The region boasted 111 collieries, of which 58 were red ash coal and 43 white ash coal.

> Seven of the red and four of the white ash collieries were not in operation during the year 1852—being new ones. Sixty-two of these collieries are working coal out above water level, and forty-nine below water level. Forty-eight of the red ash collieries shipped during the year 1852, 776,675 tons and forty white ash collieries shipped 1,520,744 tons, making a total of 2,297,419 tons. This is not the whole amount of coal shipped during the year 1852, as there were collieries in operation during that year that are not now in operation; consequently this collection does not include them.

The Reading Railroad shipped from the region 1,650,912 tons and another 800,038 tons were shipped via the Schuylkill Canal.

There are 210 steam engines employed directly at the various collieries; 3,805 horse power for hoisting coal and pumping water from slopes and shafts, the deepest of which is 353 yards and the shortest, 33 yards; 1,375 horse power for pumping water only, and 1,891 horse power for preparing the coal for market; making an aggregate of 7,071 horse power.

It was noted that the thickest vein being worked was 80 feet and the smallest was two feet.

The report stated that the amount of individual capital invested in the Schuylkill coal business was $3,462,000 (calculating with the Commodity Price Index, $80.75 in 2006 had the "purchasing power" of $3 in 1852) and that did not include money invested by landowners.

Big Money Men

Who were the wealthiest men in the area in 1865?

It should come as no surprise that the majority of the 25 men listed in an article in the August 31, 1865 edition of the *Shamokin Herald* were engaged in the mining industry or merchandising associated with it. The article, compiled from records of the county assessor's office, gave the annual income in excess of $1,000 for businessmen of Shamokin, Mount Carmel, and Shamokin Township.

The highest income was that of John Hough who managed the Susquehanna and Coal Mountain Improvement Company, which opened the Coal Mountain Colliery and Breaker in 1855. Hough, who leased the operation with a partner in 1860, had a yearly income of $21,188, which would be the equivalent in purchasing power of more than $270,000 now.

The next highest income was that of William Fagely at $19,471. Fagely, who opened Shamokin's first store with his brother, Reuben, in 1839, entered the coal business in 1841 and later leased the railroad between Shamokin and Sunbury. The Fagelys were involved in mining operations at the Gap, Green Ridge, Locust Gap, and Luke Fidler among others. At one point, practically the entire laboring class of Shamokin was employed by the Fagely brothers.

Not far behind Fagely in income was George Schall of Mount Carmel with an income of $18,814. In about 1855, Schall, with his partner Donohoe, who also was on the high income list, opened the Rough and Ready Colliery and commenced shipping furnace coal. In 1861, they took over the Coal Ridge Colliery.

Another of the five-figure salaries on the list was that of William H. Marshall at $15,785. Marshall, who came to Shamokin in 1851 as land agent for Judge William Helfenstein, became one of the most prominent businessmen of the coal region. In addition to mining, he was involved in real estate, banking, and was the founder of the Shamokin Water Company.

Other names on the list associated with the coal region include John B. Douty, Stephen Bittenbender, S. A. Bergstresser, W. P. Withington, David Heiser, and Daniel Weaver.

Aside from businesses having to do with mining, others who made the list were primarily engaged in farming. These included men like Joseph and Samuel Hoover, Aaron Burrel, George W. Snyder, and Amos Vastine. The majority of these incomes were four figures and the equivalent of less than $20,000 in today's money.

Big Project

In the summer of 1871 the Philadelphia and Reading Iron and Coal Company launched a major project involving the Mammoth vein near Wadesville, Schuylkill County.

The *Shamokin Herald* of May 21, 1874 reported vertical shafts were being sunk near the St. Clair road.

> Nothing of the kind upon so gigantic a scale has ever been before attempted in this country and the work opens to the engineers a far wider and more fruitful source of information and instruction in such matters than they were able to gather from the work upon other shafts in this country.

The Mammoth vein, considered the greatest coal bed of the Anthracite region, was believed to be between 20 and

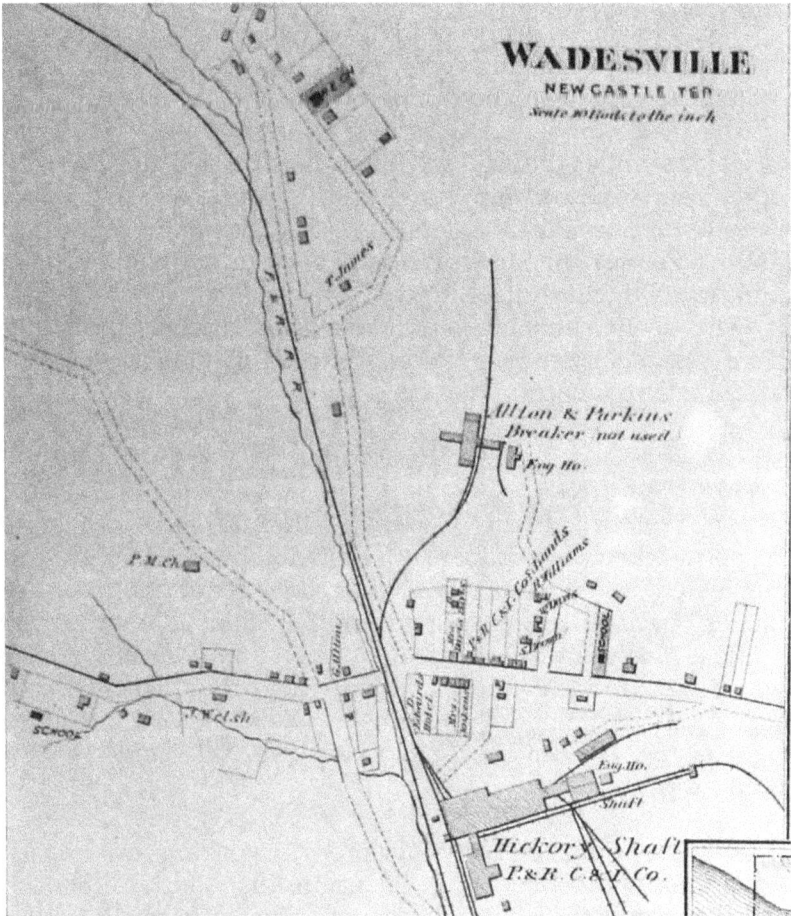

Map of Wadesville from County Atlas of Schuylkill, Pennsylvania, From Recent and Actual Surveys and Records by F. W. Beers and A. B. Cochran (New York, 1875)

25 feet in thickness in this vicinity and it was estimated the shafts would have to be sunk 1,500 feet to reach the vein.

The ground was first broken (at the site owned by the company) May 5, 1871, when it remained idle until August 3, 1871. At that time work was commenced properly upon it, and has continued since very satisfactorily to those interested. The work is of the most tedious kind that could well be imagined, from the fact that in its progress nothing but slate, rock and coal has been encountered, which is very much unlike boring through sand.

It was noted that the workmen had passed through two other veins of coal, the Tracey and the Little Diamond, and were as of May 21 at a depth of 720 feet in the east shaft and at 512 feet in the west shaft. They anticipated making another 200 feet in another week or two.

The drilling machines employed had diamond bits and were worked by steam. Small charges of blasting powder were used to a certain degree.

Mollie-Fodder

The editor of the *Shamokin Herald* was quick to respond when newspapers in Philadelphia and New York suggested in January 1877 that the treatment of slate-picker boys was a breeding ground for Mollie Maguires.

The local editor was irked by the comment and said it was unfair and the kind of "... statement that gives the coal regions a heathenish name."

The report from the *New York World* that angered him read, in part:

The sight of forty little boys working in a cold, unhealthy room at a laborious occupation for the pittance of one, two or three dollars a week is not a good one to see in this country. When we add that not more than three out of the whole number could read or write, the inconsistency of such a state of things with the safety of our republican institutions is made too plain to require comment. Children trained up in such a fashion will make good material for Mollie Maguires.

Until there is a law passed in this State compelling ignorant parents, who do not appreciate the advantages of education, to send their children to school, they will continue in ignorance; but such a law would not benefit the children throughout the coal regions alone.

Breaker boys working at the Ewen Breaker in Pittston, Luzerne County.

The response of the *Herald* editor is of a tone akin to that of Marie Antoinette about letting the poor eat cake or saying that people working for a minimum wage are happy just to be working and shows where his true sympathies lay. He called the slate-picker boys "... as mischievous and frolicsome a set of youngsters as ever dabbled in dirt."

He continued:

> Many of them pick slate from choice in order to earn their own spending money. As to their ignorance, some of the best scholars in the public schools of Shamokin have picked slate and will do it again. Many of the boys belonging to families in good circumstances have served a term in the breaker, and they do not feel degraded.

As to the miners in general, he agreed that those engaged in mining coal were at present receiving low wages and that many were, unavoidably, out of work. But, he added, "... as a rule the miner who has work is not unhappy. They may not look joyous with their dirty clothes and smut-begrimed faces, but though comparatively few

The Cameron Colliery, later known as the Glen Burn Colliery, was a major contributor to the Shamokin/Coal Township economy while it operated. The site is located along well-traveled State Highway Route 61, the main artery through Shamokin. The colliery was the largest operation along Route 61, which serves as the gateway into the anthracite-mining region of Northumberland and Schuylkill counties.

they are the happiest miners in the region, and we hope the time will speedily come when all may have an opportunity to get black faces at fair wages."

Coal Shipments

A report in the January 17, 1879 edition of the *Shamokin Times* reveals the Cameron Colliery shipped nearly 160,000 tons of coal in 1878.

The Cameron, operated by the Mineral Railroad and Mining Company, shipped 159,700 tons and was the top producer for that year in the list of 31 area collieries listed in the report. Running a close second and third were the P&R Coal and Iron Company's Mount Carmel shaft with 121,267 tons and Mineral's Luke Fidler with 103,299 tons.

Other big operations included: Henry Clay No. 1, 96,998 tons; Big Mountain, 92,837; Monitor, 88,210; Stuartville, 80,442; Excelsior, 72,310; Bear Valley, 71,933; Locust Gap, 63,970; and Enterprise, 63,414.

Other collieries on the list were Stirling, Buck Ridge, Trevorton, Ben Franklin, Locust Spring, Peerless, Hickory Ridge, Black Diamond, Lancaster, Reliance, Greenback, Packer, Henry Clay, Franklin, Geo. Fales, Carson, Marshall, Burnside, Hickory Swamp, and Helfenstein.

Total shipments of all for 1878 were 1,344,254 tons shipped by rail, which the newspaper said was down 323,909 tons from the previous year.

Outlets to markets for Shamokin coal were to Baltimore and York via the Northern Central Railway; to Philadelphia by the Philadelphia and Reading; New York via the Lehigh Valley; Erie and the Great Lakes by the Philadelphia and Erie; Elmira and northern New York by the Williamsport and Elmira Railroad; and to Havre de Grace and other points south via the Pennsylvania Canal.

An interesting side table showed the increase in production for the Shamokin Region from the commencement of operations in 1839 (a mere 11,930 tons) to 1878. Shipments had first topped a million in 1870 and continued to increase through ensuing years.

'Purely Greed'

Generally, Franklin B. Gowen and the Reading Coal and Iron Company had the support of newspapers of the coal region. But in the 1890s when transportation rates made bituminous cheaper and idled anthracite coal mines, opinions wavered.

The *Shamokin Herald* followed the lead of an earlier attack in the *Philadelphia Press* and identified the problem as "purely greed."

"The policy promulgated and carried into effect by Franklin B. Gowen is bearing its legitimate fruit," an article in the February 7, 1890 edition of the *Herald* charged. "It has not been the policy to support the market so much as it has been the policy to furnish traffic to the railroads that

Irish-American Franklin Benjamin Gowen was President of the Reading Railroad from 1870-1886. He died at only the age of 53, but had risen from moderate circumstances to control what would become the largest railroad in America by age 34, ultimately being forced from office by J.P. Morgan at age 50. In those sixteen years he had made the Reading into the largest corporation in the world, despite having comparatively little interest in and no training in railroading.

has controlled the anthracite business and brought it to its present pass."

The *Philadelphia* article contended that the capital and labor of anthracite mines had been arranged in ignorance of the size of bituminous deposits and in the mistaken belief anthracite could keep pace with their production. The *Shamokin* report argued it was not so much the competition offered by soft coal as it was the greed of the transportation companies.

Bituminous coal is driving anthracite from the market simply because the sources of supply are so scattered that one or two, or a dozen, railroad corporations cannot pool arrangements for carrying it to market. It may be that the present condition of affairs will open the eyes of the anthracite producing and hauling railroads to the folly of the policy they are pursuing.

The writer charged that the Reading had loaded itself with interest bearing debt in acquiring the title to vast coal tracts that couldn't be developed for years in addition to the expense of wages for filling great storage bins along the line and the cost of "loading and unloading and loading and unloading the cars again before it reaches the market."

It (anthracite) is the toy of the carrying companies and its market is circumscribed by the limits of their lines and interests. Its bituminous rival enjoys the benefit of competition on the part of the transportation companies. This combination must change its policy or it will, as it has nearly, quite defeat the object for which it was formed and end in utter ruin.

Turn the mines over to men who will operate them for their legitimate purpose of producing coal and with fair transportation rates they will redeem the anthracite trade and place it where a warm winter will not absolutely paralyze it as is now the case.

Group Action

Sometimes group action can accomplish what no individual can do alone.

Such was the case in the spring of 1892 when the future of Trevorton was in jeopardy.

While Shamokin in that year was experiencing a growth period conditions were desperate in the neighboring community in Zerbe Township. As with many area communities, prosperity fluctuated with that of the coal interests on which they were dependent.

Coal shipments from Trevorton in 1857 were 110,711 tons but had dropped to 62,406 by 1889. In 1892 work was stopped at the North Franklin Colliery and, according to reports in the *Shamokin Herald*, people in the community were in dire straits and there were fears the community was doomed.

Many families, deprived of income, were seeking help from the township. Others were packing up and leaving in hope of finding employment elsewhere.

In desperation, a community meeting was held and a delegation was appointed to go to Philadelphia and intervene with mine owners. The delegates succeeded in getting a three hour meeting in April with Archibald A. McLeod, president of the Philadelphia and Reading Coal and Iron Company, and C.E. Henderson, general manager.

The officials informed the delegates that there were two problems with North Franklin. First, the coal was too soft and slacked when exposed to the weather, resulting in much dirt. Second, as of the past December, more than 25,000 tons were already in stock and at least 9,000 of those tons had to be mixed with other coals to make it salable.

McLeod said he was sorry for the people of Trevorton and would do all he could toward resuming work. He said two things would help—reducing the accumulation at the yards and that output would improve normal prices, giving a fair chance for the coal to compete in the market. It was explained that Trevorton pea coal was bringing only $1.10 while pea coal from other collieries brought $1.50. Henderson also sympathized with the local people and expressed the belief that operations could resume by May 1892.

The colliery did subsequently resume operations, though the situation might not have turned around had the community not taken the action it did.

Steam Power

In these days long removed from the heyday of anthracite mining we tend to think in terms of the men and boys involved.

There is another aspect that may be of interest to some —that is, the machinery required to operate a mine. An article in the January 31, 1884 edition of the *Shamokin Herald* sheds a bit of light on that subject.

The story reported that plans were under way to add six new boilers to the steam power at the Cameron Colliery. It was noted that there were already 22 boilers in line and the six additional would make a nest of 28 boilers in one line.

At the old slope are six more. The engine at the dirt plane is supplied by three more. Four boilers are necessary to run the Rock slope engine, making a total of 41 boilers. A standard boiler is 34 feet long, making a grand total of 1,394 feet of boilers, ranging from 31 to 34 inches in diameter, not counting the locomotive boilers.

The engines consuming this vast amount of steam made by this array of boilers, are four hoisting engines, one breaker engine and three fan engines outside the mines, and two hoisting engines inside the mines. Two of these hoisting engines are double engines.

The steam is run down into the mines in pipes a distance of 800 yards to the hoisting engines, and from there, a distance of 140 yards more to run seven steam pumps throughout the mines. In addition to these are the two locomotives used on top of the dirt plane.

The article said the water used in making all this steam was provided by the Shamokin Water Company but they could not estimate the number of tons of coal consumed daily at the colliery to feed all the required fires.

And, it was noted, in addition to the enormous steam supply, 67 mules were required to assist in handling the mines and other cars before the coal was even prepared and ready for market.

Officials identified as having a part in the steam project were Holden Chester, superintendent; Thomas Steele, mining foreman; and Joseph W. Anthony, outside foreman.

Diversification

A slowdown in mining and a glut of houses available for rent brought a call for diversification of industry in 1890 in Shamokin. The situation resulted in the organization of the

Silk mill in Shamokin.

Shamokin Industrial Company later that year for the purpose of promoting the industrial interests of the community.

As early as January 17, 1890, landlords lamented in the *Shamokin Herald* that there were 50 vacant houses in town and tenants were slow in paying their rents. The article pointed out that between January 1, 1889 and January 1, 1890 the breakers in and around Shamokin were only working about half time.

"We have, in the first place," an unidentified landlord was quoted as saying, "more houses than we have people; and in the second place, we have more people than we can feed and clothe and take care of from the one industry of anthracite coal mining." He recommended the community seek to diversify its industries to provide more employment for its citizens.

"It would enable the miner to tide over the dull seasons," the interviewee continued.

Suppose, for instance, we had a silk mill. This would require a few skilled operatives to be sure and would increase the population. It would, however, give employment to the daughters and sons of the miners, who are idle.

I have among my tenants a miner who has four grown up daughters and a son. The girls are too high strung to go out to service and yet they would all jump at the chance of working in a factory. They would there become a source of revenue instead of dependents.

This unidentified spokesperson suggested that a variety of small enterprises would be better than a single large factory. He continued:

Little institutions that will give employment to a few are, in my judgment, better than those on a large scale where hundreds are employed and where a little business depression throws them out of employment.

People here maintain that a coal mine is better than all your factories, but it does not require very astute judgment to pronounce the fallacy of their views. There is no disguising the fact, and only the fool will object to the declaration, this matter of diversified industry must receive immediate attention of our people or our town will go back.

Manufacturing Town?

As a depression in the coal trade deepened in the summer of 1890, a reporter for the *Shamokin Herald* urged leaders to look to Scranton as an example of how the community could be changed to a manufacturing center.

In an article in the August 15 edition of the *Herald*, the reporter commented on an argument he overheard between a merchant, a coal and iron company official, a lawyer, and an investor.

The subject was Shamokin as a manufacturing point and the participants contended that the expense of living here was too great to allow the successful operation of factories.

Men would work cheap enough until they learned the business, and then they demand wages that employers could not pay, although the sum was not unreasonable considering the cost of living. The mines offered these people a chance to work at fair wages, and as a consequence the factory must suffer.

The merchant suggested that people in Shamokin indulged the most expensive luxuries, buying fruits and vegetables at the highest prices weeks and weeks before prices would allow residents of Danville, Catawissa, or Milton to buy them. It was also pointed out that a house renting for $14 a month here could be had for $8 or $10 at Danville and even less in Milton.

"The little group finally voted Shamokin could never blossom into a manufacturing town, so long as the mines were here to keep up wages, and the prices along the curb were 25 and 30 percent more than at neighboring points."

Later the reporter said he was on a train headed to Sunbury when he met Rufus Foster, formerly of Shamokin, who was currently secretary of the board of trade in Scranton. Foster told him, though Scranton was also a coal town, businessmen had worked together and the city had four silk mills and other factories representing a capital of $22 million and employing more men, women, and children than they did in the mines. He added that they were working to get more, negotiating then for a lace factory and a foundry to manufacture pipe.

The *Herald* report concluded by urging that a committee be formed to visit Scranton and see how they had accomplished this change. "If labor can be employed in the factories in the mining town of Scranton, it can be so employed in the mining town of Shamokin."

Breaker-Building Record

A Northumberland County breaker may have held a record for having been built in the shortest period of time.

When a fire on July 15, 1880 burnt the Enterprise breaker at Excelsior to the ground, some 260 men and boys dependent on the colliery for employment were devastated. Thomas Baumgardner of Lancaster, president of the Enterprise Coal Company, hastened to the scene.

According to a story in the *Shamokin Herald*, "... the embers were still glowing when Mr. Baumgardner viewed the scene of desolation and determined that these unfortunate people should not be idle one hour longer than the absolute necessities of the case demanded."

Following negotiations for supplies, machinery, and mechanical skill, Joseph Kaseman of Shamokin was awarded the contract for the woodwork and John Mullen, proprietor of the Shamokin Iron Works, got the contract for the machinery.

The *Herald* wrote on September 9, 1880:

The plan adopted was for a double breaker, larger than the old one. And, as one half of the old breaker had been erected in 34 days, Captain Wm. Gable, the efficient superintendent of the colliery, hoped that one half of the new breaker, though of larger dimensions, could be completed within the same space of time, and it is a matter of astonishment, therefore, that the new breaker commenced preparing coal on Friday, Aug. 27, after 27 days' work, or one month and one day after the work of rebuilding had commenced. Since Monday, the colliery has been shipping an average of about 100 cars per day.

The newspaper credited those involved in the project and speculated that "... such a breaker has never before been completed in so short a time in the Anthracite region."

Baumgardner and his brother and partner, David, drove the slope for Enterprise from 1864-65. The breaker was allegedly burned by the Mollie Maguires in May of 1875. It then burned again in 1880. After, the rebuilding, operations continued under various owners until the late 1930s. The breaker was dismantled in 1937.

Another Dream

While coal gave Shamokin its first economic prosperity, some entrepreneurs envisioned a future in the manufacture of iron.

As early as 1825, Henry Myers had erected a small charcoal furnace, which operated with bog ore found in the vicinity and charcoal prepared at the site. This operation was doomed by difficulty in obtaining limestone. The Shamokin Coal and Iron Company began turning out quantities of pig metal early in the 1840s at a new foundry. Operations were suspended on May 24, 1842 by a major fire and, a short time later, the furnace itself blew out.

In 1845 the Shamokin Furnace was sold at sheriff's sale and this again stimulated dreams of revived prosperity. The *Sunbury Gazette* of June 14, 1845, waxed enthusiastically:

> This furnace being well constructed and of a large size, capable of running about 70 tons of iron per week, and most advantageously situated by the side of the coal and ore, its present proprietor will be able to realize large profits from its operations.
>
> Shamokin will be very naturally improved by the working of this furnace. It will give employment to hundreds of persons in the mining of coal and ore. To keep it in blast will require an expenditure of upwards of $50,000 per annum. This sum distributed among the people of that place and vicinity, will give life and prosperity to the whole neighborhood.

Alas, those dreams were not fulfilled and the furnace was up for sale again in 1854. The *Gazette* reported on August 19, 1854:

> This is among the largest furnaces in the State, with an engine of extraordinary power, and all the conveniences and improved arrangements necessary for the manufacture of iron. It was erected in Shamokin about ten or twelve years ago, but did not then prosper, remaining in an inactive and useless condition until it

was transferred to the hands of the present energetic and enterprising owner. We wish him success—we hope the business he is commencing in Shamokin will become indefinitely extended until that region will be as famous for its iron as it is already for its anthracite coal.

That was not to be. The furnace ran with varied success until 1872 when it was finally blown out.

Rival Entrepreneurs

Though the Philadelphia and Reading Coal and Iron Company was the major player in coal land ownership in the area, its rich holdings attracted the envy and competition of some other entrepreneurs.

One of these—the Robert Morris Land Company— waged a legal battle with the P&R for several decades over ownership of some 8,000 acres of prime real estate between Ashland and Shamokin.

When the Morris group filed a claim in the summer of 1889, Franklin B. Gowen, former president of the P&R, dismissed it as "not worth five cents."

In an article in the August 2, 1889 edition of the *Shamokin Herald*, Gowen said the dispute went back about 18 years. He declared at the time that the Morris group demanded $100,000 in "hush money" to drop their claim. When Gowen refused to pay they erected a shanty on the property in dispute and attempted to take and hold possession.

Gowen ejected them by force, burning the house over their heads, and the party was arrested, indicted by the grand jury at Sunbury, and in order to avoid being brought to trial they entered into a written agreement never to trespass, enter upon or interfere with the possession of the land except by process of law. Then the claimants brought civil actions for ejectment in the court of Northumberland county to try the question of title, but when the cases were pressed for trial they were abandoned by the Morris people.

The Morris Company alleged that the lawyer who discontinued the suits was a fraud who acted without authority. They contended that they took possession of the land, erected houses on tracts, and placed tenants in them and that the Reading Company brought in an army of 1,000 men at an expense of $4,000 to eject the tenants and destroy the houses.

The 1889 suit was aimed at preventing statutes of limitation from shutting out their claim. It also failed.

The property comprised 25 continuous tracts, which included the Big Mountain, Fulton, Locust Dale, and Locust Mountain coal operations.

Utilizing Culm

Shamokin's culm bank is reputed to be the largest refuse pile in the world.

Whether that should be taken as a compliment is a matter of opinion. Through familiarity, many take it for granted. But, the sprawling man-made mountain can be an attention-grabber—particularly for those from out of the area who can be seen stopping their vehicles along the highway and reaching for their cameras.

In fact, because of its potential as a tourist attraction, there was talk at one point of seeking state help to develop the site as an Anthracite National Park.

Entrepreneurs despise the thought of waste and over the years many have turned their attention to means of utilizing culm to profitable advantage. What may surprise many is how long ago that process began.

An article in the Friday, January 29, 1892 edition of the *Shamokin Herald* addressed the question.

The utilization of anthracite coal dust known as culm, has been uppermost in the minds of operators and companies ever since the first colliery went into operation. Even miners, laborers, outside hands and slate pickers have wasted many hours in thinking of plans as to how the culm could be utilized, thus making rich the patentees.

Culm bank at colliery in Shamokin.

Many men in Shamokin at the present time are figuring on the problem. Thousands of dollars worth of culm goes to waste every day from the combined operations of the collieries about Shamokin, Mount Carmel, Shenandoah, Ashland, Mahanoy City, Wilkes-Barre, Scranton, Hazleton and the rest of the anthracite coal fields. Especially in this neighborhood does the culm prove more costly than elsewhere, owing to the Little Mahanoy and Shamokin creeks, with their tributaries washing tons innumerable from the banks and strewing choice farm lands, thus causing companies and operators many thousand dollars damages. [Some] Herndon farmers make it a business to visit the Susquehanna [R]iver and from its bed procure tons of the choicest kind of coal.

The article went on to note that Governor James Addams Beaver had appointed a commission in 1890 to investigate and report concerning culm utilization. Heber Thompson, mining engineer of the Girard estate, who was a member of that commission, noted: "We want to find out in what form it can be of the greatest use to the general public. In round figures there has been mined in Pennsylvania 700 million tons of coal. Of this about 10 percent, or 70 million tons, is in the form of dust or waste."

Thompson was a proponent of "sifting out" that which could be burned as a cheaper fuel. He would be pleased to see that the process has developed into an industry that flourishes yet today. Still, the prospect of finding other uses for culm continues to be investigated by inventive minds.

Fate of the Mules

For a short time my maternal grandfather George Lester Sears worked as a colliery blacksmith. Afterwards he had tales to tell of the hardships endured by his charges, which contributed to his decision to seek employment elsewhere.

It was not so much a case of mine operators mistreating the animals. After all, they were valuable and important contributors to the work. The mules endured the same dangers and difficulties as the men and boys working in the mines. The difference was that the men went home at the end of their shifts while the mules never left the premises, many being confined their entire lives in underground stables.

"Every day the Philadelphia and Reading Coal and Iron Company loses at least one mine mule," a company official told a reporter for a story published Friday, March 27, 1896 in the *Shamokin Herald*. "The average for February, however," he added, "was over double that, for in the 29 days that constituted the month 70 mules were killed in various ways."

In 1896 the Reading Company had 3,000 mules in active use in its mines. The *Herald* article reported that in the year ended March 1, 1895 the lives of 400 mules were

Mule involved in coal mining.

snuffed out. "They met death in all manner of ways. Some get squeezed between cars and die from internal injuries; others sustain broken legs and have to be shot, but the average keeps steadily on; that is one of the costs of mining."

In 1896 Dr. Samuel Haupt, a Shamokin veterinarian, had an estimated 2,500 mules to look after. Haupt told the reporter he was kept constantly busy. He added that sometimes the animals lived to be very old.

The article concluded:

One of them was recently taken out of the Draper mine after serving faithfully for 27 years without getting a glimmer of daylight. The colliery officials thought he had worked long enough and deserved to rest for the balance of his days.

But when the mule saw the sun for the first time in over a quarter of a century he became too frisky and was taken back into the mine to remain the rest of his days. He is yet alive and working steadily.

51

EVERYDAY LIFE
2.
The Patch

"Patch," in the sense we know it, is not a term one encounters outside the eastern Pennsylvania anthracite coal regions.

Not necessarily a derogatory term, it can convey a sense of oppression comparable to that evoked by the word "slavery" for American blacks. Still, a majority here have their roots in the patch. It is a vital part of our history and can as easily convey a sense of place for many.

Eighteen collieries operated in the Shamokin area and each had its patch during the heyday of mining. Some still exist as independent communities, only their names and recollections of elders recalling their history.

The "patch," as an institution, developed both as a result of the need to quickly provide housing for the workers arriving in this wild frontier region and the nature of the society they came from. Patches were not unique to this area, of course; they were prevalent throughout the coal regions.

Initially, mine owners provided housing and provisions because the workers lacked the capital to sustain themselves. In one sense, it was an added incentive, a fringe benefit, for the hordes huddling in tents and shanties while they waited to be hired. Later, when the mine owners realized the financial benefit to them, it became an entrenched, oppressive feudal system that took years to break.

Harsh as it may seem to us today, the system was not immediately recognized as abusive by the pioneer miners. In fact, some writers contend that the existence of the patches was a factor in attracting the Irish, in particular, to the coalfields. They were accustomed to the communal existence fostered by the cottier system in Ireland and feared the isolation demanded by the farming they might have pursued had they the capital. And, while mining

Shamokin, east end.

might be dangerous and life in the patch depressing, the work appealed to them and they soon developed an admired proficiency in performing it. In fact, they superseded the English and Welsh professionals who the absentee owners then moved up to management positions.

The Irish did not, as a group, begin to resent the system (though they chafed under the yoke of English and Welsh domination) until their jobs were threatened by the influx of new immigrants in the "Slav invasion" of the 1870s.

The patch had become a fact of life throughout the coal region. With rent and "pluck-me" stores adding to the flow of coin from coal, few absentee owners in Harrisburg or

Philadelphia were concerned about actual conditions in the patch.

Conditions varied little from the 1840s until the 1870s when unionism began to effect some change.

Crudely constructed duplexes—two rooms up and one down, weather stays over the cracks between the rough Hemlock sheathing, roofed with rusting tin—were the architectural norm in the patches. Renters received a minimum of crude furniture built by colliery carpenters. A community pump or convenient stream provided water. An outside privy sufficed for sanitary needs. Drafty and cold in winter and sweltering in the heat of summer, the homes offered only a modicum of shelter from the worst of seasonal conditions. Still, there was no alternative.

In the earliest days there was no other housing. Later, when a miner's wages advanced to the stage where he might have considered building his own home, he often found himself mired in debt to his employer and unable to leave. Some mine owners made residence in company housing a condition for employment. Many mines paid in script, which could only be exchanged at the company store, and miners were encouraged to buy on credit, thus being constantly kept in debt.

Even if they were able to leave, economic conditions were not favorable elsewhere. An eight-year depression struck the nation in 1842. In the mid-1850s, wild speculation in western land and railroads brought on another economic panic. Many banks, factories, and railroads failed and thousands of unemployed stood in bread lines in the nation's larger cities.

Can there be any wonder why the miner, when he was not working, was given to drinking, brawling, and gambling? A woman might have tried to brighten her grim world with cheap curtains at the windows, religious pictures on the bare walls, and a few wild flowers in a Mason jar on the table, provided she had time from the daily drudgery of caring for her family and home. The few diversions available to women centered around weddings, births, deaths, and the church.

Indeed, the mine and the church vied for supremacy in this constricted world. One offered the means to life, the other solace from its pain. The mine gave sustenance but swallowed up the man, the wife who succored him, the children they bore, and all hope for the future. For a long period, the church, both Catholic and Protestant, walked a tightrope between compassion for the miner and his family and a desire not to offend the capitalists who supported them all.

In the 1870s, as the Irish and other English-speaking miners began serious rebellion against the system, a new wave of immigrants arrived on the scene. Handicapped by language and naïve optimism, they assumed the yoke their predecessors were attempting to shake off. It was not until John Mitchell succeeded in getting the message across that coal was not Irish, Polish, or anything else, but in coal did they unite in common battle for independence.

Today, the patches that remain reflect little other than the names of this history. Refurbished older structures and new dwellings house people proud of their heritage but far removed from the more painful memories. The mines are gone and only the culm banks in the distance or skeletal remains of closed breakers stand as mute testimony to the past.

Hard Living

With all the technological advantages available to make our lives less harsh in the rigor of winter, it's appropriate to consider the ease we have in maintaining warmth and comfort in our homes.

When the first settlers arrived in what is now Northumberland County after the New Purchase of 1768, the friction match hadn't yet been invented. Fires were kindled primarily by striking flint and steel and praying that the resulting spark would ignite tinder that could be used to start some wood burning.

As noted from Dr. J. J. John's Scrap Book No. 3 at the Northumberland County Historical Society, "No iron stoves were used, and no contrivance economizing heat were employed until Dr. Franklin invented the iron-framed fire place which still bears his name."

Benjamin Franklin is believed to have invented his stove circa 1742, but it was not perfected and in common use until the 1770s. Like all his inventions, Franklin placed this in the public domain and did not seek a patent.

Quoting Dr. John again:

All cooking and warming in town and country were done by the aid of fire, kindled in the brick oven or on the hearth—pine knots or tallow candles furnished the light for the long winter nights, and sanded floors supplied the place of rugs and carpets.

Only one room in any house was warm, unless some of the family were ill; in all the rest the temperature was at zero many nights in the winter.

The friction match wasn't invented until 1827 in England and wasn't in common use here for nearly another decade. So, if the fire on the hearth went out overnight and tinder was damp and would not catch a spark, the alternative was to go out into the cold and walk to the nearest neighbor's house in hope of borrowing a brand.

Early Schools

The importance of education to early residents of the area is demonstrated by a history presented by J.J. John, editor of the *Shamokin Herald*, during a school gathering on April 1, 1874.

John noted that the first school building—a small, one-story frame structure on Dewart Street—was erected in 1837 for a school started by John C. Boyd, founder of the town, and Ziba Bird. They hired Abia John as teacher for a term of three months at $8 a month, plus board.

"During the year of 1838 the system of Public Schools was adopted in Coal Township by a small majority," John wrote.

The election was held in Cameron Township, which was then a part of Coal Township, and the school vote came from the mechanics who were then working at

Shamokin, as the people of Cameron were bitterly opposed to the Free School system.

During the latter part of the summer of 1839 they (school board) commenced putting up a two-story brick school house in Shamokin, which was completed and occupied about February of next year. It cost about $600.

John said the first teacher employed was John T. Rood of New York, but he quit after about 14 days. The district then hired Mrs. Mary Shipman, who also only taught a few weeks. They were followed by Amos Y. Thomas and Jehu John, both of whom remained on the job.

Among the earliest directors were Sylvanus Bird, Kimber Cleaver, Jehu John, James B. Porter, George Long, William Fagely, and David Billman.

About 1852, the Lutherans of Shamokin determined to create a college. A building project was undertaken but, owing to a want of funds, the project faltered and the building stood in unfinished condition for a number of years. In 1857, it was suggested that the school district purchase this College or Academy building, as it was known. There was dissent and it wasn't until March 14, 1864, that the district purchased the Academy building for $2,950 at a county tax sale.

In 1864, Shamokin became a borough and a separate school district in 1865. In 1869, the Shamokin High School was established with S. J. Barnett, a graduate of Millersville Normal School, as teacher.

On the date of John's speech, he said the district had 16 schools with 17 teachers and about 1,200 students. The district comprised one high school, two grammar schools, six secondary schools, and seven primary schools.

Father Koch's School

Father Joseph Koch is fondly remembered as Shamokin's first resident Catholic pastor. Although Stephen Bittenbender built the area's first Catholic Church in 1839 near the Cameron gap, there was no resident priest until 1866 when the Bishop of Philadelphia

St. Edwards Church with Father Koch shown on upper left.

authorized a parish for residents of Shamokin, Trevorton, and Locust Gap. Father Koch, who had served as a military chaplain in the Civil War, was appointed pastor. It was his suggestion that inspired the building of the original St. Edward's Church, and he served an incumbency of 51 years in the parish, which is now known as Mother Cabrini.

What is less often recognized is Father Koch's contribution to education in the community.

When he first came to Shamokin in 1867 he started a night school, which had at that early date more than 50 students. That led to the founding of the first parochial school in the fall of 1874. The following year, five Sisters of Charity from New York were placed in charge. In 1883 Father Koch erected a three-story school building on land opposite the church.

These would be achievements enough to warrant him respect in the educational field. But there is another even less known aspect to the story.

In the January 31, 1890 edition of the *Shamokin Herald* it was reported that Father Koch had initiated a night school to assure educational opportunities for boys who worked in area breakers and could not attend school during normal hours.

The school was organized in the basement of St. Edward's Church and 52 boys showed up for the first night. They came in response to an invitation the priest issued from the altar on the previous Sunday.

The *Herald* reported that Father Koch "wore a happy smile" when he faced the students that first night.

He delivered a short address in which he showed the necessity for good behavior and diligent attention to study; they were there for business; they must come into the room quietly, take up their books and begin to study, and when through they must go directly home; they must be careful not to give cause for complaint by the neighbors, and any misconduct would be read out in the church during the Sunday services.

Enrollment was confined exclusively to those who were working during the day and the newspaper reported that enrollment exceeded 100 boys in the following week. Few of those children might have had opportunity for education were it not for the noble priest's efforts.

The National Sport

Baseball has long been a serious concern in the Coal Region. Everyone here is familiar with the Coveleskie brothers. Some may also recall that Jake Daubert, who played for 14 years with the Brooklyn and Cincinnati clubs, was also a native of Shamokin. Then there's Walt Huntzinger of Pottsville and "Silent John" Titus, a native of St. Clair, Schuylkill County. One might also mention that LaPlume Township in Lackawanna County was the birthplace of Christy Mathewson. Pete Gray, the only one-armed man to play major league baseball, was born and raised in Nanticoke, Luzerne County.

The first clubs organized in Pennsylvania to play the game we now know as baseball were probably those in Philadelphia. The Olympic Ball Club, the first to write a constitution and slate of rules, was formed in Philadelphia in 1837. That club reigned in the city for 30 years until it was succeeded by the Athletics.

But, it might interest fans to know just how early clubs were organized in Shamokin.

The *Shamokin Herald* of August 9, 1866 reveals "That the invigorating exercise afforded by our National game of Ball is duly appreciated in this community is evinced by the organization this week of two clubs, named respectably the 'Osceola' and 'Anthracite.'"

Officers of the Osceola were: James B. Gibson, president; James B. Wingate, vice president; James E. Forrester, secretary; Thadeus Bogle, treasurer; and William A. Richardson, S.S. Clark, and Alexander Caldwell, directors.

Elected as officers for the Anthracite were: David Hodge, president; James Booth, vice president and treasurer; Francis Morgan, secretary; James T. Getter, assistant secretary; James T. Getter and Michael Larkin,

Stan Coveleski pitching for Cleveland of the American League.

field captains; and Paul Roth, John Boughner, and John Nicholson, directors.

"Both clubs contain members who, with practice, will make first-class players," said the *Herald*.

The two new clubs held their first match game on Wednesday, August 22, 1866 on Scotch Hill. The Anthracites were declared the victor when the game was called because of rain after seven innings.

L. Dewart of the Susquehanna Club, Sunbury, was umpire for that first game and scorers were J.A. Weaver, Susquehanna, and J.B. Gibson of the Osceola club.

Tri-State League

Fans in the area rejoiced in the summer of 1905 when Shamokin's premier baseball team was granted a franchise in the Tri-State League.

An article in the August 11, 1905 edition of the *Sunbury Daily Item* reported that approval was granted by league officials after they were approached in Harrisburg by a committee from Shamokin, asking for the franchise of the Coatesville team, which was disconnecting from the league.

The committee, headed by G. G. Kulp, brother of former Congressman Monroe Kulp, asked that the new franchise be granted to Shamokin instead of Reading, promising to assume bond of $500 to play the entire season and meet all conditions.

Prior to this, a Shamokin team managed by Kulp had played in the Susquehanna League and had been trounced by Sunbury, who took the pennant for the season.

The *Item* reported, "Shamokin is a rattling good ball town, has a fine park and the support of all is liberal. All of these conditions as weighed against Reading favored Shamokin, and it was decided to drop Reading, its backer agreeing to take up the coal town."

The newspaper reported that baseball enthusiasts at Shamokin were "highly delighted."

Gilbert Kulp, brother of former Congressman M. H. Kulp, principal owner of Edgewood Park, where the games will be played, departed for Wilmington (Del.) at once, as soon as he was assured Shamokin had been taken into the League to look over the team and select his players. He has twenty-two men to choose from.

It was also reported that the Edgewood team, of which Kulp was manager, would be disbanded, but three or four

Jake Daubert hit .303 during his 15 seasons in the major leagues from 1910 to 1924. This is a picture from when he was with Brooklyn of the National League.

of those players would be given the opportunity to play for the new team.

The team was to play its first game at Shamokin the following week against Wilmington.

> Previous to the game a street parade will be led by Congressman Kulp and Brother Gilbert, who was one of the chief baseball enthusiasts to induce the Tri-State Association to take in Shamokin. While the ground is one of the best in the State, it will be improved further. A bleacher seating capacity of 1,500 will be furnished.

Filling the Growler

Those who labored in area mines worked up a great thirst, as is evidenced in the number of drinking establishments available to slake that craving.

It was traditional for many miners to stop at a favorite drinking establishment on the way home from work and

F & S Brewery in Shamokin, Pennsylvania in 1920.

have their growler (the pail in which they carried lunch) filled with beer to take home.

A report in the January 10, 1896 edition of the *Evening Item*, Sunbury, reveals that Shamokin, Coal Township, Mount Carmel, and Mount Carmel Township represented two-thirds of the number of applicants for license to sell liquor in Northumberland County.

Those municipalities were requesting 247 licenses out of a total of 331 to be issued when the county convened a licensing court on January 27.

Applicants for retail licenses included Shamokin, 80; Coal Township, 47; Mount Carmel, 73; and Mount Carmel Township, 13.

In comparison, applicants from other county municipalities were: Sunbury, 18; Milton, 10; Northumberland, 7; East Sunbury, 2; Shamokin Township, 1; Snydertown, 1; Ralpho, 3; Zerbe, 10; Upper Mahanoy, 1; Little Mahanoy, 1; Lower Mahanoy, 5; Washington, 2; Jackson, 1; Cameron, 3; Delaware, 1; Jordan, 3; Gearhart, 1; and Chillisquaque, 1.

Obviously, farming didn't work up as much thirst as mining.

Of wholesale applicants, Shamokin had 13; Coal Township, 4; Mount Carmel, 14; and Mount Carmel Township, 3. The other wholesale applicants for the county were Sunbury, two; Milton, one; Zerbe, one; and Turbotville, two.

At the same time, it's interesting to note that there were only two brewers in the entire county: one in Shamokin and the other in Sunbury.

Temperance

There's never been a shortage of taverns in the coal region. Drinking was an aspect of the coal patch noted by many historians. In fact, as Wayne Broehl Jr. points out in his excellent book, *The Molly Maguires*, that alcohol was actually sold at many collieries up until the 1850s when public pressure put a stop to the practice.

This is not meant as a slur on the miners. Few laborers in history have lived and worked under such austere conditions for so long a period. The tavern was one of the few social outlets available where the miners stood equal to one another and could relax after a hard and dangerous day of work.

Since drinking was so pervasive in that society it may come as a surprise to discover that the temperance movement was active here long before the days of Carrie Nation and her famous ax.

A lengthy article in the August 31, 1865 edition of the *Shamokin Herald* urged support for abolishing the sale and consumption of alcoholic drinks.

Fifteen years ago there was [sic] some 60,000 pledged total abstainers from all intoxicating drinks in the State of Pennsylvania. Now, alas! There is [sic] less than 8,000. The demon of intemperance triumphs. Hundreds —yes thousands—in our midst are yearly hurried to a drunkard's grave, to a drunkard's hell, and shall we sit still and do nothing?

The writer noted that there were two total abstinence societies in Shamokin—the Sons of Temperance and the Temple of Honor—and urged the public to join them. Both organizations were founded in the 1840s and quickly spread throughout the U.S. and parts of Canada.

Illustrating how important some considered them, the Sons of Temperance had an initiation fee equal to a week's wages of an ordinary worker. Both were secret fraternal organizations with signs, passwords, and rituals.

Influenced by Dr. Benjamin Rush of Philadelphia, the first temperance society in America was formed in 1789. The American Temperance Society was organized in 1826 in the wake of a renewed interest in religion and morality. The goal of all these organizations was total abstinence and, eventually, led to the Volstead (Prohibition) Act in 1920.

Bathing in the Creek

It was illegal to bathe in Shamokin Creek—at least within Shamokin Borough limits and certain time limits—in the 1870s.

This was among a number of ordinances reenacted by the new borough council and included in a report in the April 17, 1873 edition of the *Shamokin Herald*. The report gave this information on the ordinance:

All persons are forbidden to bathe in the creek within the Borough limits after six o'clock in the morning and before seven and a half in the evening, under a penalty of Fifty Cents for the first offense and One Dollar for the second, and so on, the penalty increasing One Dollar for every subsequent offense. On Sabbath not at all.

Council also cracked down on persons allowing goats, swine, horses, mules, or cattle to run at large, imposing fines of from 50 cents to $5, or forfeiture of the animal.

They cracked the whip even harder in regard to dogs. They imposed a tax of one dollar for the first, two dollars for the second, and so on for all dog owners. Persons who declined to inform the assessor of dogs in their possession were to be subject to a fine of five dollars.

Because of the fear of rabies, it was illegal for owners to allow any dog ("unless securely muzzled") to run at large during the months of June, July, and August.

Council also enacted a fine of two to five dollars on the disturbing of peace and harmony, "... such as crowds blocking up streets, sidewalks, etc., or hallooing, using profane, vulgar or obscene language."

A fine of one to five dollars was also set for failure to remove coal ashes and rubbish from city streets and sidewalks, and from $10 to $20 for failure to remove nuisances, "... such as sink holes, water ponds, privy vaults or other nuisances or offensive matter of any kind or description, detrimental to the health or comfort of the inhabitants of this borough."

Buffalo Bill

Buffalo Bill Cody, showman, Pony Express rider, buffalo hunter, and American Indian fighter, played Shamokin with one of his earliest traveling shows in 1885.

While visiting the Buffalo Bill Museum and Grave several years ago in Colorado I saw the ledger with the troupe itinerary and noted their visit here. I now know they arrived in Shamokin for a show held on Bunker Hill.

Louis Poliniak wrote an article on this same subject for the *Citizen Shopper* of September 15, 1976. In that article he said the exact date was unknown, but he believed that the show came to Shamokin in 1883 under the auspices of the Lincoln Post GAR.

The museum records actually state that the visit was on December 9, 1885.

Buffalo Bill traveled with five different troupes during his show career. The visit to Shamokin was by the original Combination acting troupe, which was on the road from 1876 to 1886. This was among the earliest visits by this troupe to the coal region. Prior to Shamokin, the troupe played Hazleton on November 28 and Wilkes-Barre on December 7, 1885.

Buffalo Bill Cody.

The troupe came to Shamokin aboard the Northern Central Railroad and the cars were unloaded at the old Shamokin Fair Grounds between Market and Sixth streets. Tents were then pitched on Bunker Hill where the performance was held.

According to Poliniak's article, Coleman Sober of the Sober Chestnut Farm in Irish Valley challenged Cody to a shooting match. Sober, a world champion marksman at the time, defeated Cody and several other challengers. Annie Oakley, another expert shot, joined Buffalo Bill in 1885 but there is no indication that she was involved in Sober's challenge.

With his show, Buffalo Bill took a sampling of American frontier life around the world from 1872 to 1916. Zane

Grey, who began his writing career in Pennsylvania, was the last person to interview the old scout before his death in 1917.

Cody made nine visits to Pottsville between May 1873 and May 1916. But let the record show—he was in Shamokin before he visited many other area communities. And this may be the only place where he was challenged to a shooting match and lost.

Blue Laws

Controversy over current legislation to remove Pennsylvania's ban on Sunday hunting is a reminder of how restrictive the commonwealth's blue laws once were.

With the exception of hunting and car sales, the laws enacted in 1794 have all but disappeared in Pennsylvania. Less than a century ago, they still forbade most any "work or toil" on the Sabbath.

In the fall of 1890, Lawrence Little, a Shamokin ice cream merchant, dared to challenge the law. Arrested for violating the law, Little decided to stand trial. The *Shamokin Herald* of October 10, 1890 reported on his hearing the night before in the offices of Squire Rowe.

> Word had been passed along the line, and when the trial began the office, the hallway, the stairway and the street in the neighborhood were crowded with anxious humanity, representing both sides of the question.
>
> Lawyer Gillespie represented the prosecution and Lawyer W. W. Ryon the defense. Witnesses were examined, and weighing the evidence thoroughly, Squire Rowe decided that Little was guilty as charged. He fined him $4 and cost, which he refused to pay and an execution was issued and given to a constable to levy on his property.

Little's lawyer applied to the court for a writ of certiorari, which would stay the execution. If granted, it would also bring the case before the court for trial.

The *Herald* commented:

Meanwhile the opponents of the Sunday law have not been idle, and the prospects are that they will meet and organize to defeat the enforcement of the law. It is proposed, in order to accomplish this to insist on its strictest enforcement. This will shut out the Sunday newspapers, close up the livery stables, and prevent people from driving about in their own conveyances for pleasure on Sunday.

It may come as a shock to some younger readers to realize it wasn't until 1933 that the laws were eased enough to allow baseball and other sports to be played on Sundays. And, despite the fact that the state Supreme Court ruled them unconstitutional in 1978, the blue laws remain on the books.

Cake Walks

What was billed as the "grandest cake walk since the foundation of Shamokin" was hosted on June 19, 1883 in Douty Hall.

Reporting the event on June 21, the *Shamokin Herald* said, "The long expected, long looked for, and longed for cake walk, under the auspices of the colored folks of Shamokin, came off in Douty Hall on Tuesday night, and to say it was a complete success is putting the matter very mildly."

Many historians believe the cake walk originated among slaves as a means of satirizing the culture of supposedly "superior" whites. Be that as it may, the events became popular throughout the country and were a fixture in minstrel shows through the late 19th and early 20th centuries.

Though the black population of Shamokin was never large, some elements of unwarranted racism may be seen in the reporting. For instance, naming of the white judges of this event had precedence over that of the participants and winners of the contest and the reporter expressed "surprise" at the excellence of the speech by the organizer.

A cake walk in the 19th century was a strutting dance in which walkers who performed the most accomplished or amusing steps were awarded a cake as prize.

Participants in this Shamokin event were Charles Wallace and Mrs. Sadie Carr of Harrisburg; John Williams and Mrs. Sarah Lee of Pottsville; Miss Costly (first name not listed) of Sunbury; George Miller and Mrs. Talbot, Shamokin; Henry Tarr of Shamokin; Mrs. Regie Roberson of Gordon; and "... others whose names were not learned."

Wallace and Mrs. Carr were the grand prize winners. Second prize went to Joseph Wilson of Pottsville and Mrs. A. Gordon Jones of Shamokin.

The cake was received on behalf of the winners by Mr. Jos. Wilson, who was in Shamokin for the purpose of establishing a secret order of colored people. His speech surprised the audience by its excellence and entitles him to a place among the orators of the day. He was complimented by tremendous applause.

Judges for the event were W. H. Douty, Colonel Alex Caldwell, Major James May, William Beury, George Marshall, E. C. Fourl, and William H. Talbot.

Spelling Bees

It may not seem very entertaining to us in our jaded society, but spelling bees were a favored source of fun for our ancestors—and not just for children.

A case in point is found in a report in the May 20, 1875 edition of the *Shamokin Herald* on the first spelling bee of the season held at the Academy of Music under the auspices of the YMCA.

Ivanhoe S. Huber and Harry Shissler were appointed captains, each choosing 11 for a total of 24 spellers. R.T. Owen served as pronouncer and C.P. Helfenstein, G.W. Ryon and W.W. Evert were judges. After spelling around several times, the judges reported 19 words missed on Shissler's side and 20 on Huber's.

The editors of the *Times* and *Herald* were called onto the teams, the former with Shissler and the latter with

Huber. It was decided that the first six spelled down would be contestants for a leather medal.

Mr. S.P. Fink was given the first word—'menagerie' but he didn't succeed in the show business and stepped behind the scenes. 'Ratiocination' was not reasoned upon correctly by Messrs. Shissler and Morganroth and they went to console Mr. Fink. Mr. A. J. Gallagher didn't fasten 'cleat' properly and of course could not hold out any longer; Mr. Wm. Zimmerman found 'impermeable' too large for him and the editor of the Times, D.D. Domer, went up on 'effervesee.'

These gentlemen constituted the leather medal class. Spelling down then progressed rapidly until but five were left—Mr. Huber, Mrs. Col. Alex. Caldwell, Misses Mary Ramp, Lillie L. Evert and Belle McEliece. Mr. Owen exhausted his list in reducing these to two— Mrs. Caldwell and Miss McEliece. The latter going down Mrs. C. was first best for the evening, but before leaving the stage she gave us to understand she didn't know all about 'ichthyology.' The Shamokin creek is certainly a poor place to study it.

Fink left before the spell-off. Morganroth withdrew after a couple rounds and Zimmerman went down soon after. Finalists were Shissler, Domer, and Gallagher; Domer won the medal.

Interestingly, only one child took part in the event— Johnie Withington, who the judges reckoned to be about the best speller of the evening. "The pronouncer ruled axle-tree wrong because the hyphen was not called out," wrote the editor of the Herald. "This was the first we ever knew that this little mark belonged to the alphabet or entered into the orthography of words otherwise than as a mark of division in compounds."

Tramp Trouble

On the morning of Monday, February 6, 1882, police raided an encampment of tramps under the Shamokin Bridge. Three men were arrested and held for court.

Society—and especially law enforcement—viewed tramps as undesirables: men unwilling to do honest labor and prone to criminal acts. A series of economic crises in the 1880s and 1890s increased the number of transients traveling the country, particularly by riding the rails, in search of temporary employment. Contemporary newspapers contain many accounts of crimes attributed to tramps.

A story in the February 10, 1882 edition of the *Northumberland County Democrat* on the criminal term of court commented on the three arrested in Shamokin, saying they were: "... very malicious looking persons, and judging by the company they keep, the good people of Shamokin have reason to congratulate themselves that they are in jail."

During the raid, police testified, a brother of the "notorious Pat Lawless" and several other known criminals fled the scene. It was suspected that they sought to have the tramps join them in a burglary or other crime.

Witnesses said the tramps had arrived in town on Saturday, February 4, and begged their bread until Monday. The three men plead guilty to charges under the tramp law then in force. The court sentenced George Brown to nine months, James Atkins to six months, and Thomas Rogers to one month in jail. The newspaper explained that the court was more lenient to Rogers because he had been ill.

An arrogant tramp caused a ruckus in Shamokin one night in November 1885 until he was taken into custody and given a night in jail.

The account in the November 28, 1885 edition of the *Shamokin Herald* did not give the offender's name. It recounted that on the evening of November 18 the man was intoxicated and begging on the streets.

When the man continued his panhandling in the C.A. Barron & Co. drugstore he was approached by William Booth, a local mine superintendent. Booth told the man that there were plenty of collieries about the town where he could find work.

The tramp, who claimed to be from Hazleton, replied he wasn't a laboring man and if he couldn't get his living by asking for it he would steal it.

Constable Haley was summoned and told the man if he didn't desist he could be arrested. The bold tramp told Haley that if he was arrested he would revenge himself by burning down the town.

With that threat, Haley took the man into custody and charged him before Squire Erdman. In lieu of $500 bail, the offender was taken to the lockup.

Suspicion and fear of tramps continued well into the 20th century. In 1906 one scholar estimated the number of tramps in the United States at 500,000, or about 0.6 percent of the nation's population. In 1911 the *New York Telegraph* cited that study and reported that the estimated number had increased to 700,000.

Rabies

Rabies, a virulent infection generally spread by the bite of an infected mammal, remains a threat in the U.S. and around the world. Though the number of deaths is small compared with the rest of the world, the disease has increased in the United States since the 1970s, with the majority of cases attributed to bites by raccoons, skunks, and bats.

The fearsome aspect of the disease is most familiar to many from the films *Old Yeller* and *Cujo*.

Imagine how much more frightening the disease was in the days before Louis Pasteur and Emile Roux developed the first preventative vaccine in 1885.

There are many examples in early area newspapers of rabies epidemics and cases to illustrate just how fearful it must have been. One such case was reported in the June 30, 1875 edition of the *Shamokin Times*.

A man named William Horn of Doutyville sold a gun and a dog to Francis Weikel, who lived about a mile from him. The dog had been a pet in the Horn home and was taught to perform several tricks, which delighted his children. Several weeks after the sale, the dog returned to Horn's house. While the children were playing with it, the dog snapped at 5-year-old Alfred Horn, its teeth cutting into the skin of his left hand and drawing four drops of blood.

Since the injury did not appear to be serious and the dog showed no obvious symptoms, no one gave it much thought. A few days after the dog was returned to its new owner, it began attacking Weikel's chickens. He caught the dog and penned him up in a stable, but in doing so the dog bit him on the wrist.

"The dog also began to snap at boards and sticks in the stable," reported the *Times*, "and then his owner began to suspect that the animal was mad and so he was promptly killed. Before being penned up the dog had bitten Mr. Henry Updegrave of Doutyville."

Two weeks after the incident at the Horn residence, little Alfred fell ill and Dr. Emerson Farrow of Taylorville was summoned. "As soon as he had examined the child he informed the parents that he feared the boy exhibited symptoms of hydrophobia (rabies) and inquired whether the boy had at any time been bitten by a dog."

Though the parents had considered the wound trivial, the doctor's opinion was soon confirmed by the rapid decline of the child who only lived another five days.

"Mr. Weikel and Mr. Updegrave, both of whom were bitten by the same dog, naturally feel apprehensive of what may possibly be the result in their cases," concluded the article.

Breaker Model

Though surrounded by mines and breakers, not everyone who lived in the coal region in the 1870s was employed in the industry.

For that reason, two enterprising machinists built a working model of a breaker and mine that was exhibited throughout the region to familiarize the public with the mining of coal and its preparation for the market.

An article in the December 26, 1879 edition of the *Shamokin Times* announced that the model of the Black Diamond Breaker and Mine was then on exhibit in the Kutzner & Douty building.

No description that we are able to give would do justice to the remarkable little coal breaker and the mines attached to it, and we would therefore recommend our readers to go and see it for themselves. All who have seen it yet have been surprised at the ingenuity displayed in the mechanism of these little coal workings and all pronounce the exhibition as one that is worth far more than the price of admission.

The project was the handiwork of William Y. Thomas, who was employed as a machinist in John Mullen & Co.'s Shamokin Iron Works, and George Pettigrew, a machinist in Dickson's Manufacturing Co., Scranton.

The newspaper said Thomas originated the idea of the model while working as a slate picker at the Black Heath Colliery in Schuylkill County. Both men were working in Dickson's shops at Scranton when they began the project in June 1870. It took nearly six years of working in their spare time to complete the model. "Both the men were poor and they had no means to aid them in the production of this remarkable piece of mechanism," the *Times* said.

The breaker model was 9 feet high, 15 feet long, and 5-feet, 6-inches across the chutes. The newspaper noted, "The breaker is operated by a little engine of 3-inch bore and 5-inch stroke. The same engine operates the mines attached to the breaker."

The breaker was described as perfect in all its working details.

On the platform are three figures, representing men engaged in raising gates, shoveling coal into the breaking rolls and breaking large lumps. Coming down the steps to the screen room are several boys loafing, as is always the case around a breaker. In the screen room is a slate-picker boss pacing to and fro, with a stick over his shoulder and a pipe in his mouth. The slate pickers are busy and are being closely watched by the boss. There are sixteen figures altogether on the breaker, all busy at something.

The mine operation also included moving figures, including a balky mule and various machinery. "The full number of figures at work on the breaker and around the mine is 34—all dressed in the costumes natural to the work in which they are engaged and all moving about or busy doing something."

One wonders where this marvelous model is today.

Vacations

We don't often think of our ancestors taking vacations but, in fact, some did. So, where would an area resident have gone on vacation in the 1870s?

An article in the *Shamokin Times* of August 15, 1879 provides one possible answer for that question.

Many persons from Shamokin are anxious to take a run out of town for a day or two during the warm season, and it may not have occurred to them that one of the most pleasant little excursions in this neighborhood is a trip to the Switchback Railroad and Glen Onoko, near Mauch Chunk.

Railroads popularized the southern end of the Lehigh Gorge as a resort area beginning in the 1870s. The Hotel Wahnetah at Glen Onoko offered 47 rooms, a dance pavilion, tennis courts, carriage and horse rides, and guided hikes to the falls. By the mid-1880s tourists were coming from as far away as Philadelphia and New York. The hotel was closed by a fire in 1911 and another in 1917 ended the resort era until 1980 when the area became part of the state parks system and again began attracting tourists. Mauch Chunk (now Jim Thorpe) was then only a switching point but is now a tourist attraction in its own right.

The 1879 newspaper article noted:

Arriving at Mauch Chunk, coaches are in waiting to take the tourist to the Switchback, and getting on board one of the little open cars in use there you are

Mt Jefferson Incline, Switch Back Railway, Mauch Chunk Car departing, pushed by barney. Barney pit and special rails in foreground (from the Switch Back Home Page).

taken over the mountains without locomotive and with no annoyance from dust or cinders. The scenery along the Switchback is grand in the extreme and must be seen to be appreciated.

And that was only the beginning. Commenting on Glen Onoko, the writer continued:

At this beautiful and romantic spot there is much to interest everybody and four hours are soon passed in viewing the Chameleon, Onoko and Cave Falls, Packer's Point,&c. Beautiful walks guide you up the mountain side and at frequent intervals are comfortable seats where the excursionists can rest. The air in the Glen is quite cool even on the warmest day and ladies find extra wrappings of use.

The article emphasized that the whole trip up and back could be made in 14 hours and "... there is no short excursion in this vicinity that is so full of interest as the trip to the Switchback and Glen Onoko."

Most Popular Sport

What was the most popular sport in the coal regions and across the nation in the last half of the 19th century?

No, it wasn't football.

Pedestrianism, or distance walking, was America's most popular sport until the late 1870s when it lost out to baseball, football, and other "new" sports.

The sport came to America in February 1861 when Edward Payson

Edward Payson Weston

Weston—who might be called the father of the sport here—walked from Boston to Washington to settle an election wager. After completing the 400 mile jaunt in his proposed 10 days and winning a bag of peanuts, Weston proposed other distance walks to break existing British records and found promoters happy to put up prize money. This attracted other athletes to compete against him and one another.

In addition to distance races, which were followed by referees, timekeepers, and spectators on horseback and in buggies, competitions were held in arenas and drew large crowds. A popular variation was the "go-as-you-please" race, which combined walking and running.

The popularity of the sport here is evidenced in contemporary news reports. One such was found in the July 10, 1879 edition of the *Shamokin Herald*:

> The feature of the day (a July 4 celebration in Mount Carmel) was the eight-hour 'go-as-you-please' between Chisnel of Ashland and Quinn of Minersville.

At the stipulated time, 11 o'clock, both men appeared on the track and walked up to the stand where the judge and scorers were seated. Capt. Wm. F. Huntzinger, of Shamokin, was chosen judge; James Getter, of Shamokin, and B.F. Horan, Esq., Mt. Carmel, as tally keepers.

At the word 'go' both men struck out on a lively walk. During the time they were making the first mile it was nip and tuck for the first pole. Quinn, however, succeeded in keeping the pole. Amidst applause both men passed the mark side by side, having completed their first mile in 9.35.The second mile they kept close until the 11th lap was completed when Chisnel gained a lap. From this time it was quite evident Chisnel had everything his own way.

At 1:20 o'clock (two hours and 18 minutes from the time they started) Major O'Brien of Shenandoah, Quinn's trainer, stepped up to the judge and announced that Quinn conceded the race; that he had taken a pain in the side.

The Minersville men lost heavily. Patrick Duffey and John Donahoe were the heaviest losers. The former lost two hundred and the latter ninety-five dollars.

Unfortunately, it was the prevalence of gambling that diminished the luster of the sport and helped fuel its demise.

Pigeon Shoots

Though a controversial matter in more recent times, pigeon shoots were a popular sporting event for our ancestors.

A match that drew a large crowd and heavy betting was reported in the May 20, 1875 edition of the *Shamokin Herald* and pitted David Whitehouse of Pottsville against Richard Eisenhart, a younger contender from Shamokin.

The match took place near Shamokin and attracted a crowd of about 200 spectators. "Not a few backed their suppositions by betting heavy and about half that number, who were miners, think some of the shooting was a little too close (to the birds) to benefit them financially."

Whitehouse, a 50-year-old miner, had a wide reputation as a shooter and was regarded as among the best in Schuylkill County. Eisenhart, 26, also a miner, "... has but recently entered the shooting arena and consequently has not the experience of his opponent, but within the last few days he has shot 15 birds out of 15 which had a tendency to inspire his friends with confidence in his abilities."

Whitehouse took the match, winning by four birds and claiming a stake of $400.

Mr. Eisenhart's friends claim that he did remarkably good shooting, having made but one clean miss. They also contend that he was not shooting at common birds, as Mr. Whitehouse's experience and facilities enabled him to select very small and quick birds, thereby placing Mr. Eisenhart at a disadvantage, he not being accustomed to shoot at any but common country birds. Mr. Whitehouse is death on birds.

Fireworks on the Fourth

The Fourth of July was equally a holiday for our ancestors and it might be of interest to examine how they celebrated the day on the eve of the nation's centennial.

The *Shamokin Herald* reported on July 8, 1875 that the community observed the holiday on Saturday, July 3, in a "very quiet manner," noting that the day was "pleasantly cool and nothing occurred to mar its enjoyment that we could learn."

The newspaper said nearly all the local Sunday schools held picnics and Camp 149, Patriotic Order Sons of America, sponsored a parade. Participating were Camp 149, Camp 30, POS of A, Shamokin Cornet Band, American Mechanics, and the Shamokin Guards.

Though there was no mention in the newspaper, other reports of July 8 make it clear there were fireworks.

The big celebration in the community was on Sunday when pastors of various Protestant churches sponsored a united religious and patriotic service in the Academy of Music. According to the report, the hall was crowded.

Rev. Dr. W. Lee Spottswood, pastor of the Methodist Episcopal Church, was chairman. He said the object in coming together was "... to have a grand religious and patriotic celebration of the 99th anniversary of the nation's birth in which all could participate and in which God would be honored and praised for our many and great national blessings."

After prayer and music, Dr. Spottswood opened the floor to speeches, which were limited to 10 minutes. Reverend Dr. W.S.H. Keys, pastor of the United Brethren Church, made the opening speech, declaring, "There is too much gunpowder burnt and not enough of God in our Fourth of July celebrations." He said he didn't favor this manner of celebrating and called for a reformation.

When the chairman opened the floor to remarks from the audience among those who responded was C. F. Joy, who disagreed with Dr. Keys. He said he believed in the firecracker method and didn't think it advisable to turn the day into one of devotion and speech-making. "There should be something in which all could engage," he declared, "the little children as well as the adults."

Insurance Mania

Insurance is considered a prudent and necessary investment today. In the 19th century, when there was no unemployment compensation or social program to assist injured workers or their widows and orphaned children, it might seem equally reasonable that the public would have been favorable to insurance.

Surprisingly, there was a period in the 1880s when even the church and those who might have benefited from coverage looked askance at insurance and considered it speculative at best and evil at the extreme.

A report in the Thursday, June 2, 1881 edition of the *Shamokin Herald* detailed a convention of the Pottsville District of the Evangelical Church held at Shenandoah where the ministers adopted several resolutions condemning what they termed the "insurance mania."

They approved one resolution, which called the insurance business "speculative," "wild-cat," and "... fraudulent and wrong in principle and demoralizing in its effects." They also resolved "that we earnestly entreat all our people to shun and discourage said business as a public evil, hurtful to the church and to the State, as well as to the individuals engaged therein," and requested "the Legislature of our grand old Keystone State to pass a law forbidding this nefarious traffic."

Among the ministers attending that convention were Reverends Henzel and Shoemaker of Shamokin; Kemble and Rinker of Shenandoah; Leopold of Mahanoy City; Sands of Schuylkill Haven; Saylor of Pottsville; Hess of Ashland; Worman of Frackville; and Reitz of Cressona.

Evidence of similar opposition to insurance can be found relating to other Protestant denominations and the Catholic clergy.

The opposition didn't discourage those who recognized the need, though their good intention often fell prey to overly zealous expectations.

One example of that was the Henry Clay Mutual Aid Society organized in Shamokin in 1881. It lasted all of 14 months before going bankrupt after the tide of public opinion cut off the flow of revenue to meet expenses.

"Many of the assessments that were sent out were never heard of more," said the *Shamokin Times* on April 29, 1882, "and it was beyond the bounds of all possibility to keep the society afloat under such adverse circumstances ... She went up the flume, kicked the bucket, cracked her nozzle and busted her last trace."

Gas Lighting

While we consider electric lighting the ultimate in illumination and cite with pride Thomas Edison's sojourn in Northumberland County, it did not win supremacy over other forms without a struggle.

An article in the Friday, October 17, 1884 edition of the *Shamokin Weekly* demonstrates that area gas companies did not give into their competition easily.

"That the gas companies do not intend to yield their territory in illumination to the electric light companies without a struggle is being manifested in other ways than a reduction in cost," the article stated. It was noted that many improvements were being made in quality and adaptability of gas lighting.

One of the most successful of these is the Siemen's gas burner for illumination of stores and large buildings. It is of shape somewhat like an hour glass, the illumination being at the waist. They are made of various candle powers, and give a strong but soft light which with the aid of a large white shade affords great brilliancy over considerable ground.

One of these burners has just been put in Morganroth & Co's dry goods store by the Shamokin gas company and is giving full satisfaction to the firm. Its cost in the consumption of gas is very much less than with the ordinary burner, as it is claimed for it that burning at full power of 500 candles it will consume only 50 feet of gas per hour, where the same light in the common burners would use up 140 feet of gas. Its expense is thus brought down to about ten cents per hour, a figure which electric light companies will with difficulty get under.

Whether in cost or other conveniences, we acknowledge —and are thankful—that Edison's invention did finally prevail.

Mail Delivery

We take such things as free delivery of mail for granted today. But it didn't come to pass in Shamokin until December 1890.

Before that, people were obliged to go to the post office to pick up their mail.

Announcement that free delivery had been approved for the community was made in the Friday, October 10, 1890 edition of the *Shamokin Herald*. Institution of the service required that postal business of a community exceed

$7,000 for the year closing on the preceding March 3 and that population be in excess of 5,000. Shamokin met both requirements and the newspaper article said that postal business for the year was expected to reach $10,000.

However, concern was expressed about another requirement.

> It is learned from a reliable source that Uncle Sam will not turn his mail carriers loose in a town or city until the houses are all numbered. There is no mistake about this. The people of Shenandoah were nearly losing its benefits from this very reason. An inspector may be expected here any day, now, and if he finds the house number missing he will submit an adverse report and then the order will be withdrawn.

City council resolved to enforce a number ordinance, but the newspaper still expressed concern.

> This action, however, will amount to nothing unless the property owners are agreeable, as they may, by becoming puffed up with their individual rights, decide to test the matter in the court, and during the slow process of litigation the opportunity will pass away.

Without the delivery option, the *Herald* called the post office "... as great a nuisance as can be found in the town." Prior to institution of free delivery, the newspaper would advertise a listing of people with mail at the post office and they were required to go there to pick it up.

> There is a perfect crush of people there each evening, and men, women, and children are compelled to stand in line and wait for a chance at the delivery window until patience is sorely tried. Under the delivery system this will disappear.

Postmaster Simon Wagenseller urged the public to be more careful when mailing letters and packages. He noted that many letters were placed in the office without stamps and without the writer's address on the envelope. The price of a stamp at the time was two cents.

The *Herald* article concluded:

> It is now learned that there are a large number of people here who will not take a letter in which they suppose a bill is enclosed, from the office, while others, after opening, will drop them back in the box as opened by mistake. A very cute trick.

Dance Feud

Though we view it as a social and recreational activity, dancing was the basis for a feud that began in 1896 in Locust Gap and was not resolved for another 39 years.

Often condemned from an opposite perspective, the ancient roots of dance are religious—tracing the movements of heavenly bodies, propitiation of crops, and celebration of military victories. It is much more recently in history that dance became a recreational pursuit.

One of the more unusual aspects of dance is as a competitive event, and nowhere was it practiced in that sense more than in the Anthracite coal regions at the turn of the 19th century. With limited options for recreation, dance took on the form of a contest of skill, agility, and perseverance, complete with gold medals, cash prizes and, of course, heavy betting.

George Korson, dean of Pennsylvania folklorists, tells of this particular competition which began in 1896 at Locust Gap.

In that year, Patrick "Giant" O'Neill of Shenandoah, reigning champion, was challenged to defend his title against George "Corks" Kramer, a youth from the Gap. O'Neill's nickname was based on his superiority and not his slight stature, while Kramer's reflected the lightness of his step.

After an exhibition of Hibernian jigs, clogs, and reels, dance forms with roots deep in Gaelic tradition, Kramer was declared the winner. O'Neill's supporters cried foul, claiming prejudice on the part of local judges, and refused to respond to offers of a rematch with a $2,500 wager.

Years passed, but they did not lighten the bitterness.

Finally, in 1935, an invitation was issued for the pair to settle their feud by dancing in a competition at the Pennsylvania Folk Festival in Allentown. Both men agreed.

After watching the pathetic exhibition between two gray-haired, stooped, short-winded old men, the embarrassed judges agreed to call a draw.

To their credit, the two ancient rivals were men enough to shake hands and call a truce, which won them an outburst of cheers and applause.

Football

Football is the supreme sport throughout the coal region. Say you don't like the game and you run the risk of becoming a social outcast.

But in 1894 a Methodist minister from Philadelphia took that risk and condemned the sport as "brutal, a gambling game and, above all, un-Christ-like." His comments were published in the Wednesday, December 12, 1894 edition of the *Evening Item*, Sunbury.

Reverend George R. Graff said he had previously played the game, supported the team while attending Hackettstown Seminary in New Jersey, and even attended the previous Thanksgiving Day game between Harvard and the University of Pennsylvania. But his opinion changed after reading an article in the *Christian Advocate*, which convinced him "... it was not a game but rather a battle of selfish rivalry."

He cited statistics revealing that 23 young men were killed playing the game in 1891, 22 were killed in 1892, and 26 were killed in 1893, a total of 71 in three years. In addition, he said, there were 121 legs broken, 23 arms, 54 collarbones, and 158 other injuries in the same period.

"This is as high a percentage of hurts as an ordinary battle would show. One man was killed in a prize fight in 1893, 26 in football."

Aside from the aspect of physical injury, the pastor noted:

Gambling. It is said that $50,000 changed hands during the Harvard-Yale game. This is one of the principal objections to prize fighting. Ought it not to apply to football?

Second, one great and well-founded objection to the game is the dissipation in which the students indulge after it is over, all too well known to need elaboration.

Again, football serves no sufficiently useful purpose or ideal. It is popular because Americans are fond of intense action in everything. Would not the same energy be better employed in elevating mankind and in the suppression of vice?

While opposed to the game, the minister said he had great respect for the players who he called "the best and grandest fellows in the world." Still he concluded football was "... out of harmony with the spirit of the age, and expect to see it speedily replaced by some better game of development and amusement."

Needless to say, he didn't get his wish.

Barking Curs

An increasing number of dogs in the community raised the ire of a reporter on the *Shamokin Herald* in the spring of 1890.

In the May 2 edition he lamented:

When the moon hath climbed the mountains and the stars are shining too, a little mongrel cur in the northeast corner of nowhere will catch a glimpse of his shadow and let out a bark that echoes from Bunker Hill to Cameron culm bank and from Big Mountain to the township school at the head of Shamokin [S]treet.

It is then the midnight curs take up the refrain, with a little bow-wow here and a bigger bow-wow there, and a great big bow-wow over yonder. This tremulous canine chorus that awakens the ambient air into contortions will generate more sulphurious sin in an hour among a sleepy populace than the churches can neutralize in weeks and months of solid labor.

He noted that the assessors had recorded the number of dogs with owners in each ward as follows: First ward, 211; Second, 102; Third, 150; Fourth, 113; Fifth, 107; and Sixth, 109, for a total of 792 whose owners could be fined for disturbance of the peace. However, the reporter added, the situation was aggravated by:

> ... tramp dogs, that have no owners or visible means of support, within the borough, and are fully equal to the number of those upon the assessment rolls, from which it may be ascertained the volume of bark and yelp, and snarl and growl that is sent out to infest the people when the moon is bright.

But the reporter wasn't done yet. He had still another complaint:

> The cow with a bell. She is just coming out, with the green grass in all the vigor of spring freshness. A man in the suburbs thus relates his experiences: I was just dropping off to sleep the other night when from the distance came the tingle-lingle-ling of a cow bell. On it came, nearer, and clearer, deadlier than before. The tingle-lingle-ling was changed into a clang, clang, clang as with measured tread and slowly Mrs. Bovine drew up beneath my window and let out a trinity of moos that drove dull leaden heeled sleep from the premises.

And More Noise

A recent survey by the non-profit Noise Free America found that noise levels in metropolitan areas have risen six-fold in the past 15 years. And the racket from sources including increased traffic, lawn mowers, chainsaws and other loud tools, pounding-bass auto stereos, and recreational machines has been found to be detrimental to health.

Studies show noise can increase stress, raise blood pressure, and cause depression, hearing loss, and lack of sleep.

Though there is no national noise policy, complaints are forcing some communities to toughen codes.

But, this is nothing new.

Complaints about noise and ordinances to limit it go back centuries.

An illustration of this is a letter to the editor in the Friday, September 7, 1888 edition of the *Shamokin Herald*.

"I think it was an Englishman who is credited with having given the name of 'American Devils' to steam whistles, a very appropriate appellation for the article of which Shamokin must certainly be the centre," the contributor wrote. "Every locomotive that enters the town— the number is legion—gives vent to all the noise it contains."

But the writer wasn't done there. He added:

> ... every businessman who possesses an engine as a labor saving machine, immediately erects a 'chime whistle' with which he entertains the community three times a day much to the disgust of people with nerves and heads. This might be overlooked since it gratifies the owners of the chimes so much to hear them frequently, if it were not the way they cling to the value of the Cameron and other 'chimes' at the hours of 4:30 and 5:30 in the morning. Considering that this is a town of some 15,000 inhabitants the percentage must be comparatively small who are desirous of being awakened at these hours every morning. If Shamokin continues adding chime whistles, the inhabitants will be so hardened to noise that the sound of Gabriel's trumpet will scarcely surprise them.
>
> The latest lunacy is sounding the fire alarm at six o'clock every evening, but I suppose, this is only to gratify a whim of another 'chime' crank, hence must be endured.

Epidemics

More than 30 people died when an epidemic of diphtheria and scarlet fever swept through the community of Locust Gap in the late winter of 1892.

Locust Gap Station on the Philadelphia & Reading Railroad.

This, of itself, was not an unusual situation in those days before improvement in medicine. What is unusual is that, rather than addressing housing conditions, authorities put the blame for this particular epidemic on the people, particularly "foreigners."

A contagious and life-threatening disease, diphtheria is now rare in the United States because of widespread immunization. It has always been most common in areas where people live in crowded conditions with poor sanitation.

In 1892, many of the houses in Locust Gap were owned by the Philadelphia and Reading Company and, as was typical in mining patches, they were built close together. Some residents complained to the company that the cellars of many houses had filled with drainage water. They believed the germs that cause the ailment had developed in this stagnant water and caused the epidemic to take root.

In response, George M. Medlar, district land agent for the P&R went to Locust Gap along with a Dr. Barto, president of the Board of Health of Mount Carmel Township, and James McCarty, secretary.

Reports in the *Shamokin Dispatch* and the *Sunbury Weekly* in early March make it clear that weather conditions made it impossible for the inspectors to make a thorough investigation. However, the Sunbury newspaper noted:

> ... sufficient evidence was revealed to leave no doubt in the minds of these gentlemen that if six months ago the citizens would have believed that 'cleanliness is next to Godliness' its population would not have been so greatly decreased.

While the inspectors conceded that some cellars did contain water, they attributed blame for the epidemic to the habits of the residents. The *Dispatch* contended that:

> Inquiry revealed the fact that it was customary for the inmates to throw their refuse water a few feet from the back door and then cover it with ashes. A better breeder of sickness could not be prepared and it is remarkable that more deaths did not occur.
>
> Some of the residents of Locust Gap are foreigners and it was in their colony that most of the dirty piles of rubbish, ashes and other breeders of disease were found.

Though they felt the worst of the disease had abated, the inspectors said they would return for another inspection.

Despite vaccination campaigns beginning in the 18th century, smallpox also remained a threat and inspired fear throughout the 19th and into the 20th century in the United States. One instance of that fear was noted in the spring of 1892 when 28 cases were reported in Schuylkill County.

An article in the April 8 edition of the *Shamokin Herald* urged the borough's board of health to be alert and take measures to guard against smallpox "... stealing its way into town." It was reported that the western end of Schuylkill County and the whole of the Williams Valley were affected by an outbreak of the disease.

A young man who was employed at Tower City visited his home at Lehighton, Lehigh county, some weeks ago, and while there papered a room in which a patient afflicted with that much dreaded disease had been lying, and which room was, no doubt, infected. Returning to Tower City he was stricken with the malady and died. The people of that place are doing their utmost to stay its spread by quarantining, the employment of nurses and the assistance of the medical profession.

Eli Kauffman and William Shade, both of Tower City, were appointed as a committee to oversee obtaining proper medical assistance and temporary quarters for persons suffering from smallpox. On arriving in Pottsville to meet with directors of the Schuylkill almshouse the two reported that they had received $50 in donations and made arrangements with area merchants for necessary supplies.

They noted that 23 persons had been quarantined and two fatal cases had already occurred.

After successful vaccination campaigns throughout the 19th and 20th centuries, the World Health Organization certified the eradication of smallpox in 1979.

Prejudice

Prejudice never goes away, though the identity of the victims changes with time.

The point is made in numerous articles through the years. Race or religion weren't always the qualifying factors. Mere difference is enough to warrant suspicion.

This is evident in Benjamin Franklin's warning about German "aliens" who he feared would gain prominence over the English-speaking populace:

And since Detachments of English from Britain sent to America, will have their Places at Home so soon supply'd and increase so largely here; why should the Palatine Boors [Germans] be suffered to swarm into our Settlements, and by herding together establish their Language and Manners to the Exclusion of ours? Why should Pennsylvania, founded by the English, become a Colony of Aliens, who will shortly be so numerous as to Germanize us instead of our Anglifying them, and will never adopt our Language or Customs, any more than they can acquire our Complexion. [4]

A more recent example was an article in the *Danville Sun*, which was copied by the *Evening Item* of Sunbury on September 29, 1897. The report was a commentary on a record-breaking 300 cases on the docket for Northumberland County Court, which necessitated bringing in a judge from Lycoming County to assist the local jurists.

The newspaper charged that the majority of the persons involved in the court cases were foreigners—Poles, Lithuanians, Hungarians, and Italians. "They are an illiterate set, quarrelsome and pugnacious," the newspaper said, "they resort to the law on the slightest provocation, hence it is a rich harvest field for lawyers."

The writer added:

A large share of them pay no taxes to the county, being aliens. It was hoped that the law taxing aliens passed at the last session of the State Legislature would compel this class to pay a slight tax to the State, but it has been pronounced unconstitutional.

It is a curious condition of affairs and a very dangerous one that is slowly but surely working the demoralization of society.

Bet Their Wives

It's common knowledge that love of sport can take some individuals to extremes.

---

4   Observations Concerning the Increase of Mankind, 1751.

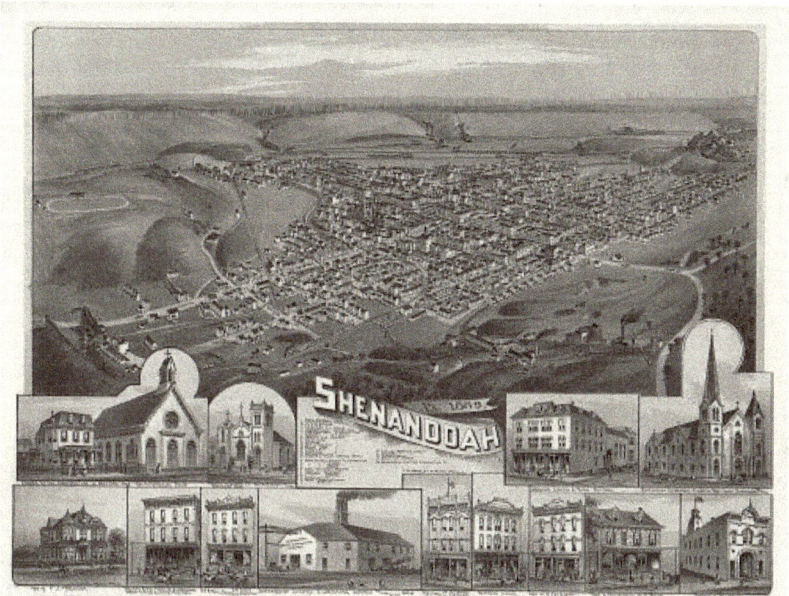

Shenandoah, 1889.

Few, though, would dare allow their sporting fever to take them to the length it did two enthusiasts in Shenandoah in the summer of 1905.

A 100-yard foot race between Alexander Klemis, a young tailor from Shenandoah, and John Derish, a crack sprinter from Mahanoy City, drew one of the largest crowds on record to the borough.

Klemis, who was trained by Martin F. Fahey, a noted Schuylkill County sporting man, defeated Derish. The race was run after a heavy rain but the *Sunbury Daily Item* reported on August 19 that Klemis ran the distance in 10 ¾ seconds.

Klemis received a purse of $200 for his victory.

What makes the race stand out in history, though, was not the distance or speed of the participants but a side bet wagered by the two enthusiasts. Anthony Norkiewich and Joseph Troskosky bet their wives on the outcome of the race after having put up all the money they could raise.

The *Item* reported:

Norkiewich, who backed Klemis, insisted on taking Troskosky's wife with all earnestness, but Mrs. Troskosky clung to her husband for protection, entreating him to undo the wrong he had done her.

To avoid a pitched battle, friends of both men interfered and adjusted things amicably, Troskosky promising to pay Norkiewich a sum of money and to 'stand treat' for a select crowd. The affair caused great excitement for a time.

One can only wonder how the enthusiasts fared with their spouses in future.

Bewitched

On the evening of Thursday, May 8, 1890, Henry Latshaw, a miner, living at Fidler Green and employed at Hickory Ridge Colliery, ate his supper, left his house, and nothing more was heard or seen of him by friends and family for the next eight days.

When he did return, the 40-year-old man told a strange tale of being mesmerized and made to wander against his will for those eight days until the spell was finally broken.

His family subsequently told a reporter for the *Shamokin Herald* that Latshaw had been bewitched by a woman with whom he had disputed religion.

Latshaw told the reporter he had started out to take a short walk after supper on the night his adventure began.

He was seized with an irresistible desire to keep on his journey. His mind was perfectly clear, but to save himself he could not retrace his steps. He had no objective point in view, but was compelled by the unseen agency to walk straight ahead.

The morning light of the following day, after a night of journeying over the mountains, through the valleys and across swamps and forest tracts, found him near Catawissa. On, and on, and on he journeyed eastward to and through Luzerne county; through the coal field operated by Eckley Coxe, but yet making no application for work, simply carried along by an indefinable power which he could not resist.

His family explained that there was a young woman who had come to their home on various occasions and argued religion. One evening:

> ... the woman went over to brother, who was setting in one corner of the room, made a few passes about his head, tapped him on the shoulder, when Henry jumped to his feet and, although he has no learning, began quoting scripture and defending the religion of the woman. The woman, after he finished his defense of her belief, read a few passages from St. John and departed.

They said after that incident, Henry began acting strangely and claimed he was under an irresistible power. "I don't know whether there is anything in mesmerism or not, or whether it is the devil," a brother said, "but I do know that Henry has never been himself since."

Henry said he had continued his journey to Williamsport and from there to Milton, Northumberland and, finally, Sunbury where the spell was broken. He then purchased a ticket for Shamokin and returned home.

When asked for the identity of the mesmerizing woman, the family said she had since moved away.

Water Woes

There's a tendency to take water for granted these days. All one has to do is turn on the tap and, generally, there's assurance of a steady supply. In the past when most people were dependent on wells and cisterns, an extended dry spell was cause for concern.

An example of this was seen in an article from the September 3, 1894 edition of the *Evening Item*, Sunbury with a headline proclaiming "Water is very scarce."

"The continued and severe drought is not only causing farmers and mine operators heavy losses, but is also productive of much suffering among the working people in different sections.

In the coal region the worst conditions are apparent. Two large collieries were shut down, owing to the lack of water several days ago and the miners were thrown out of work. The families procured their water from wells but these have been dry for days and there is today practically not a drop of water in the neighborhood.

The newspaper reported that a few people had large cisterns and in the beginning shared their supply with neighbors. "But soon finding their supply diminishing they then refused to allow anyone to go near the precious liquid except members of their own family and they only used it for drinking purposes."

As far north as Wilkes-Barre it was reported that the situation was the same.

Those who have wagons are hauling barrels full from the river two miles and are selling it at ten cents a gallon, but the majority of the miners have not a cent and it will be a week or ten days before they get their monthly pay and they cannot buy the precious water.

In many other mining villages the same condition of affairs exist, and the people are praying for water. It is feared, too, that if rain does not come soon contagious diseases will break out. Already there is a great deal of sickness, especially among the children and another week of dry weather may find the suffering reaching to a deplorable extent.

The *Item* added that the drought was not restricted to Pennsylvania as similar conditions were being reported across the country. Farmers said fields were drying up, resulting in loss of corn and other late crops and damage to fruit trees. Mountain brooks and creeks were also diminished and there were many reports of wood and brush fires.

"Fortunately," the reporter wrote, "the water supply to this city is sufficiently large to furnish all that is necessary here for some months."

View of Mt. Carmel, PA.

Brawlers

Boxing has a long and mostly honorable history in the coal regions. But a bout between two brawlers from Shenandoah almost precipitated a riot in Mount Carmel in 1892.

The contest with four ounce gloves between fighters named Gibson and Donohue for a purse of $800 attracted to the borough nearly 2,000 spectators from throughout Schuylkill and Northumberland counties and as far away as Reading and Philadelphia.

"Some were old men and rich, others young and poor, many wearing diamonds, others wearing patches on their pantaloons," reported the *Shamokin Herald* on July 15, 1892. "Plenty had private flasks and a few private parties, demijohns, but one and all had a roll of greenbacks to place on the gladiators."

Because of the drinking and general rowdiness, officials were worried and the borough council held a special session and determined that the fight should not take place within the borough limits. It was feared that this decision might provoke more trouble. After consultations between authorities and managers, permission was granted for the fight to proceed.

Before the fighters even entered the ring so many brawls had occurred and so much noise generated that Officer Hinkle jumped on the stage and demanded attention. He told the crowd if order was not restored he would call on his deputies to "clean out the place." Though there was doubt that the police could have prevailed as the crowd had come to see the fight and good money had been wagered; some estimated that the stakes were above $7,000.

Finally, the fight commenced and went on for six bloody rounds, Donohue getting the worst of it.

"The contest was fast degenerating into a slugging match when Officer Hinkle leaped on the stage and stopped the contest, amid howls of derision and rage," the *Herald* reported.

Gibson was the freshest of the two and would have likely won had the fight lasted another round.

His friends knew this and yelled 'jobbery.' They said the police had been notified to stop the fight if Donohue stood any chance of defeat, but this is not so. It was a square go and the managers deserve the thanks of the sports in being able to secure the authorities to allow the fight to go on as long as it did.

It lasted until 4:00 and was one of the prettiest, fiercest contests ever seen in the State and the most extensive yet taking place in Central Pennsylvania. The referee called the fight a draw. Most of the money was wagered on rounds. The fight will be resumed in the near future.

Closing Controversy

In this age of convenience when we shudder at the thought of a store or other business closing before midnight it may come as a surprise to learn that Shamokin merchants once contemplated the idea of shutting their doors at 6 p.m.

Petitioned by their clerks and with the proposal endorsed by the local newspaper, 15 merchants agreed to the plan in the summer of 1892. According to a Friday, July 1, 1892 edition of the *Shamokin Herald*:

> There is every indication that within a short time most of the stores in Shamokin will close at 6 o'clock. This is proper. It is very confining in stores these days and if people cannot make their purchases from 7 o'clock in the morning until the above time it is very strange.
>
> Residents should encourage this movement all they can by making all purchases in the day, and speak encouragingly of the movement, which is a popular one to the backbone.

Merchants agreed to close their stores from July 1 to October 1, 1892 at 6 p.m. and said they would not, under any circumstance, allow a customer to enter after that hour—Saturday nights and Reading (railroad) pay nights excepted.

The clerks (in the above mentioned newspaper article) requested residents of Shamokin to patronize merchants who signed their petition. "While other wage-workers are persistently agitating the reduction of hours of labor from 10 to eight hours, we trust that the public will sustain us in our reasonable demand of a reduction of two hours, from 14 to 12."

Merchants who signed onto the petition were: George W. Weitzel, T.W. Laubenstein, E. Brennan, L. Little, A. and G.W. Fagley, T.B. Hertzog, Mahlon Scholl, W.H. Zaring, D.W. Erb, J.S. Zimmerman, Burd and Rogers, J.A. Wert, and H.C. Hoover. In signing, the merchants added a condition that they would continue only on the condition that they be joined by all stores of the community.

Among the clerks signing the petition were Agnes Kohlbraker, Maze Cronmiller, Jennie Walker, Maud Shipman, Mame Walker, Belinda Corcoran, Ella Herb, Annie Glassic, Jennie Schenkweiler, Carrie Ketner, Libbie

Reed, Annie Kokinsky, John Downey, Frank Christ, Henry Kohlbraker, Bella Ludwig, Mollie Sterling, C.F. Christ, William A. Seitz, S.G. Fagely, Claude Gaskins, Blanch Roth, and George F. Fagley.

Animal Fights

A sport popular throughout the Anthracite coal regions and much of Pennsylvania in earlier times would be viewed less favorably today.

The fact that it was illegal then as it is now did not prevent many from wagering thousands of dollars on the bloody outcome of fights between chickens, dogs, and other beasts bred for the purpose.

A front page story in the March 30, 1892 edition of the *Sunbury Weekly* reported:

> Sporting men through the Schuylkill, Columbia and Northumberland counties are busily engaged these days discussing the probable outcome of the great cocking main which is to take place in the neighborhood of Shamokin some time this week.
>
> There have been numerous mains in the above named counties during the winter for small amounts of money and as one succeeded the other, the sport grew more popular, until today it has as many followers as the cranks seated on the bleachers howling when the hitter lines a base ball for one or more bases.

A follow up article in the *Shamokin Dispatch* revealed that the event was held in an old barn near Weigh Scales and the competition was between birds from Shenandoah and Shamokin.

> During the past month word was passed along the line that the fight would take place near Shamokin on Thursday, the 31st instant. A few outsiders learned of the facts and told their intimate friends. If the police knew of the approaching contest they made no sign. Parties desiring to witness the main were somewhat afraid of being arrested, but on making known their

fears would be assured by the managers that the coppers would not interfere.

The article said people came on foot, by carriage, and "the greatest number left Sunbury on the 10:20 Pennsylvania train, three coaches being packed." The event was billed as the "greatest fight ever witnessed in the Coal Region."

As soon as the preliminaries were arranged the fight began. A Shenandoah bird and a Shamokin bird were thrown into the pit by the trainers and they lost no time in getting together. The first round was short and decisive, the Shamokin bird cleaning the Shenandoah representative up in a few moments. Money was freely bet on the result of each round and the Shenandoah backers at the end of the seventh bout, which again favored Shamokin, were out over $2,000. One man from Danville took $700 out of the pool, he being the biggest winner.

Verhexed

The scams of a local psychic were exposed in the summer of 1899 by Shamokin and Sunbury newspapers.

A story in the *Shamokin Herald* was picked up by the *Sunbury American*, revealing how Mrs. Emma Jones, who resided on Mineral Street in Shamokin, "... is coining money which flows from the palms of our superstitious rich and poor alike, who are anxious to look into the future or desire to have certain persons 'verhexed.'"

The *Herald* said Mrs. Jones had spies about town who sought out new arrivals, particularly young female domestics, and gained knowledge of their past. "When the girls visit the woman, and they invariably do, they pay Mrs. Jones the sum of 50 cents and she astounds them with revelations of their past life. The future is dead easy to read."

The *American* added:

Shamokin is not the only town that has been hoodooed by this Mrs. Emma Jones, as scores of people from Sunbury have journeyed to Shamokin to especially consult this so called fortune teller. Great things have been told our people by the woman and some of her firmest believers and greatest admirers live right in this town.

The *Herald* contended that Mrs. Jones practiced not only fortune telling but also witchcraft.

Not long ago a woman went to the place and after paying the usual fee inquired into her husband's actions. She was told he was unfaithful to her. When she reached home a quarrel ensued and a lawsuit resulted. Before the justice the wife admitted that Mrs. Jones told her. She was also brought before the squire and admitted her guilt.

Another case reported is where a husband deserted his wife in town. She went to the woman and paid $1 for his return. He didn't go back to her and the witch doctor, it is alleged, said that for another $1 she would cripple him for life, according to the desires of the woman. However, the proceeding was unnecessary as the next day he returned home.

The *American* interviewed a "well known attorney ... who was consulted with the view of bringing proceedings against the alleged hex." This authority pointed out that Pennsylvania had laws against witchcraft until September 23, 1791 and it was usually determined by ordeals that were no longer permissible, such as throwing them in water to see if they might float—a certain sign of guilt.

The Library

Though the community didn't get one until 1953, the need for a public library was voiced nearly a century earlier.

An editorial in the March 15, 1866 edition of the *Shamokin Herald* is a case in point. The writer said:

Shamokin public library.

If the town is to be made attractive to the rising population, and if strangers are to be induced to settle among us, we must make use of all proper efforts of this character.

A place that is lacking in facilities for gaining information can never hope to compete with other places whose influential people give their children and others the means of personal, intellectual culture. People may come here to make money, and stay for a few years; but we can never hope to have a solid, stable, attractive population unless there be opportunities for proper mental development.

The writer of the editorial was not without a plan for meeting the goal, either. He suggested that a three-story building be erected. The first floor would be rented for stores or offices. The second floor would be used to house the library and the third floor would be a lecture hall. He proposed that rent of the stores would pay a good percentage of the library expenses and said occasional lectures by popular speakers would fund the rest.

He felt a membership of 150 persons who contributed about $3 annually would keep up the supply of papers and periodicals and add some new books.

Unfortunately, his library plan did not bear fruit.

There was a fund drive for a library before World War II, but the war interfered with those plans. It took a major campaign headed by the Shamokin Woman's Club and a number of other concerned citizens and organizations to realize the dream, which finally resulted in the opening of the Shamokin-Coal Township Public Library on September 21, 1953. The institution remains a vital factor in boosting the cultural and educational level of the community.

Wedding Squabble

Coal region weddings sometimes took a rowdy turn in days gone by.

One example of this was found in the February 14, 1902 edition of the *Sunbury American*. To avoid embarrassment of any living descendants, I'll refrain from using the surnames involved.

It seems a man named Louis had gone to a Coal Township wedding, accompanied by his wife, their daughter, and son-in-law.

> There was drinking and a big time generally as is usual on such occasions, and during the midst of the festivities Louis took twenty cents from the pocketbook of his son-in-law, which called forth remonstrance from the daughter. A squabble ensued which was shortly settled and the four people, who all live together, went home.

That might have been the end of the story. But the daughter couldn't leave it rest.

While the family was at supper, the daughter again brought up the subject and upbraided her father for his "attempted theft" and for his drinking. The father responded by throwing a plate at the girl. Another fight resulted and ended with the daughter having her father arrested on charges of assault and battery.

The case was quickly settled and they went home again in good humor, the father promising to change his ways and even offering to buy a gift for his daughter to make up for his previous behavior. They went to bed, agreeing to forget their differences of earlier in the day.

The father apparently brooded on the matter. During the night, he got up, procured a pocket knife, went to the room where his daughter and her husband were sleeping and plunged the blade twice into her side.

Fortunately, the wounds did not prove fatal. Louis was arrested and taken to the county jail in Sunbury to await the results of his attempt upon his daughter's life.

DANGER DOWN BELOW
3.
A Dangerous Enterprise

There is ample evidence that mining was a dangerous enterprise, particularly for the younger workers.

Just how dangerous may be illustrated by perusing mine inspector's reports for just one month in 1883. The following information was culled from reports published in the *Shamokin Herald* on Thursday, October 25, 1883.

In the Shamokin District there were 27 reported accidents for the month of September 1883 and seven of those resulted in fatalities. Those killed were: Thomas Tyeck, 14, a driver, died of injuries received when he was run over by the dirt dumper at the Henry Clay Colliery; Alfred Hepler, 17, driver, run over by loaded mine cars in Summit Slope, Williamstown Colliery; Odius Long, 15, driver, struck and crushed under pole of top counter chute, Mahanoy Colliery; Thomas Cook, 51, fall of slate in Short Mountain and Lykens Valley Colliery; John Dewalt Jr., 14, run over by dirt dumper at Williamstown Colliery; Andrew Martin Row, 18, driver, run over by mine cars, No. 3 slope, Williamstown Colliery; and John O'Neil, 20, laborer, fall of coal, Merriam Colliery.

There were three deaths out of 18 accidents in the Shenandoah District in the same period. Killed were Patrick Garvey, 21, laborer, injuries incurred by fall of slate at Cuyler Colliery; William Biernstiel, 17, laborer, explosion of boilers at Primrose Colliery; and James Cosgrove, 50, miner, fall of top coal in breast of Packer No. 3 colliery. While the others were unmarried, Cosgrove left a wife and eight children.

The Pottsville District reported one death in five accidents. Killed was Frank Spotts, 13, a slate picker, who died of injuries when he was caught in the chute of Palmer Vein colliery No. 1.

Life Held Cheap

Life was cheap in the Anthracite coal regions in the 19th century,

Just how cheap is illustrated by an article in the Saturday, May 6, 1882 edition of the *Shamokin Times*, which recounted accident claims paid out by Dr. J. J. John, agent for the Travelers Insurance Company of Hartford, Connecticut.

Though the list details the variety of injuries experienced by miners at area collieries and the compensation paid to them, more than half the article is devoted to extolling the virtue and generosity of the Travelers. "The work shows that the Doctor has faithfully represented an honest company—a company that stands without a peer in the history of accident insurance," crowed the article. "No assessments follow its insurance— no doubts or uncertainty about the payments of its claims."

The highest claim noted in the list was $1,000 for the death of John Fox, who was suffocated by steam at the Cameron Colliery. The family of W.H. Lott, killed by carbureted hydrogen, or "fire damp," at the same colliery, received only $375. Why there was a difference in the amount paid for death is not explained by the article.

Payment for other injuries incurred at the Cameron varied greatly. Enos O. Edmunds received $130 for an injury to his foot; Francis M. Bixler got $70 for a broken leg, and Henry D. Foulds was granted $20 when his leg was hurt by a drill, while Francis M. Bixler received only $2.14 for injuries incurred in a fall of coal. My own great-grand-uncle William Charles Fisher merited only $3.57 for an injury to his elbow (he was killed in another accident in 1902).

Payment for injuries at other area collieries also varied. Families of Peter Tabo, Pennsylvania Colliery; William Reynolds, Addison Klase and Richard Morris, Henry Clay; and Peter D. Eby, Lykens Valley, each received $250 for fatal injuries.

The largest numbers of payments recorded in this article were for injuries at the Cameron and Henry Clay.

Thirty-eight accidents were listed for the Cameron, two of which were fatal. The Henry Clay had 35 accidents, including four deaths.

The tally for other collieries was:

Luke Fidler, 12 injuries; Pennsylvania, 21, including one death; Mount Carmel, 14; Big Mountain, 25; Stirling, 15; Morris Ridge, four; Enterprise, four; Excelsior, nine; Peerless, three; Buck Ridge, two; Carson, two; Lykens Valley, 16, one death; Summit Branch, two; Locust Gap, two; Big Mine Run, five; Centralia, five, and miscellaneous, five.

The most paid out for non-fatal accidents were the $130 to Enos Edmunds for his foot injury; $90 to J. Edward Smith at Mount Carmel, injured in the fall of a top; $65 (half of claim) to Jacob Sharer, whose back was broken at the Stirling; and $60 to Condy Cunningham, who fell down a chute at Big Mine Run.

A Tax to Help the Miners

Not everyone in a position of influence took the plight of the miner for granted in the 19th century, though.

The *Shamokin Herald* reported on February 27, 1891 that Representative Elias Davis of Schuylkill County was traveling throughout the coal region, seeking support for his bill to levy a tax on coal lands for a fund to help injured miners. The *Herald* said the bill had been brought to a second reading in Harrisburg.

Davis contended that the bill was not a slap at coal operators but a means of providing for the families of men killed or injured working in the mines. David told the *Herald*:

The Girard Trust received $97,000 in royalties from the William Penn Coal Company last year and all the tax they pay to the county for those lands is $300. They kick at being compelled to do that. The Girard estate derived $517,000 from their coal lands last year.

It is such a rich trust that the directors are worried to find a way to spend the money. Yet not one cent does it contribute to the people who are hurt in their mines or to families who are deprived by accident in the mines of their means of support.

Davis' bill proposed a tax of one cent per ton on all coal taken out of the mines. He noted that 40,665,152 tons of anthracite coal were mined in 1889 in Pennsylvania.

Now if a tax of one cent a ton had been levied on that amount there would have been $406,651.52 put into a fund for the benefit of the men who risk their lives to make the rich man richer. Even if only one-half of a cent was levied, the fund would have been quite large.

However, he lamented, his bill did not seem to be winning much support among the coal operators.

I was talking the other day to a man identified with the Girard estate. He seemed very kindly disposed toward the miner and workingmen generally, but when I asked him what he thought of the bill to tax coal lands, he replied that was an entirely different matter. You see, they sympathize with the workingman, but not to such an extent as will effect [sic] their money bags.

Some things never change.

A Familiar Complaint

The complaint that Philadelphia and other large cities are better treated than smaller communities by the state legislature is not new either. An article in the February 15, 1891 issue of the *Shamokin Herald* lambasted legislators for reducing appropriation for the Miners' Hospital at Ashland.

Senator Charles J. Monaghan of Schuylkill County had presented a bill seeking an appropriation of $94,000 for the hospital. The legislature reduced it to $62,000 while increasing subsidies to various facilities in Philadelphia.

4100   MINER'S HOSPITAL, ASHLAND, PA   PUBL. BY P. H. LOEPER.

"This is in keeping with the treatment the anthracite coal region receives on all sides," the *Herald* said.

Its communities are made up of wage workers. The rich treasures of the land are sold, the profit goes to Philadelphia and other centres of wealth; the pittance earned by the toilers is all that remains here except the privilege of caring for the poverty that envelops in its mantle of despair, the old age of the miner or the helplessness that may be thrust upon him in youth or in the full flush of manhood by the lurking danger that ever stands at his elbow.

It was reported that the state had been scandalized by the story of the death of a miner named Paul Chilock. But the newspaper pointed out an examination by officials exonerated the Ashland Hospital managers from blame and revealed that the man had to be sent away to save the lives of other patients because the state had not provided funds needed to build an isolation ward.

The newspaper cited increased allotments for a Philadelphia institute for the blind, another for a training school for feeble minded children, and another for the deaf, but was most offended by an appropriation of $110,000 for "the feed and care for the vicious creatures in the Philadelphia House of Refuge."

Even the rum-soaked bummers and crooks and thieves in the shadow of Philadelphia's palatial residences receives more consideration than the poor miner who takes his life in his hands and goes down in the dark cavern and works and toils and dies it may be that the palace over yonder may be built and maintained in its luxury and splendor.

Grind them down ye heartless corporations! Subsidize legislatures to aid you in starving and subduing them!

Natural Disasters

Nature, when she chooses, can unleash devastation beyond the imagination—as was shown when Katrina and its sister storms pummeled the Gulf Coast in 2005. Imagine how much worse it was in days past when modern resources were lacking.

Such an incident occurred on Tuesday, June 2, 1862, when a severe storm burst upon Schuylkill County and then settled into a steady, heavy rain that continued without stopping for 36 hours.

Reports in the *Miners Journal, Shamokin Herald,* and other area newspapers revealed that the downpour brought the Schuylkill River and its tributary streams over their banks by the next afternoon, submerging railroad tracks, filling cellars, demolishing homes and businesses and sweeping away bridges.

The *Miners Journal* termed it the "... greatest freshet known here since the flood of 1850, which destroyed a large amount of property."

A report in the June 10 edition of the *Shamokin Herald* said St. Clair was completely isolated with the waters sweeping through the main and adjoining streets, destroying dwellings and leaving many homeless.

Collieries throughout the county were drowned out and operators reported many mules that were in the mines were lost. Hundreds of canal boats were also lost.

The damage wasn't confined to Schuylkill County. A dam at Mauch Chunk (Jim Thorpe) was swept away, taking out the railroad bridge and demolishing many houses. "The whole town of Weisport is washed away," said the *Herald*. "There are but three houses left out of about three hundred. Many families were drowned. The loss of life has been terrible."

Authorities said canal navigation was stopped for the season and the Lehigh Valley Railroad would not be in running order for several weeks.

Cave-In

The men and boys engaged in coal mining went to work daily facing the possibility they might not come home at the end of their shift.

Hardly an issue of any newspaper from the earliest days can be read without finding account of some fatal accident. The most prevalent and dangerous risk to the miner was a fall of coal, slate, and rock from the roof, ribs, and face of a chamber.

Mine inspectors' reports of Pennsylvania show that during the year 1887 there were 313 fatal accidents in or around the mines of the anthracite district. Of this number, 147 were due to falls of roof and coal, while only 21 were caused by explosions of blasting material.

One such incident was reported in the Thursday, July 10, 1879 edition of the *Shamokin Herald*.

The men composing the day shift for No. 10 slope at the Cameron Colliery in Shamokin on Tuesday, July 8, found the gangway closed up by a fall from an old breast. The men of the night crew—William McCollom, Charles McCollom, Archibald McPherson, Henry Fisher, and Edwin Edmonds, a driver, with his mule—were all shut in. The men from either side of the obstruction found they could converse and it was learned that none of the party were injured and the air was good.

William McCollom, a married man with three children, lived on Second Street. His brother, Charles, 19, lived with him. McPherson was also a married man. Henry Fisher was married with one child and lived on Mulberry Street.

Edmonds, a boy of 17, lived with his parents on Dewart Street.

Thomas Steele, the inside boss, set a crew to work in an effort to liberate the trapped men, which they succeeded in doing in about six hours. It was subsequently learned the night crew had gone to work about 6 p.m. on Monday and the slide occurred at about midnight. In all, it was estimated, they were trapped for 12 hours.

Edmonds later told a reporter for the *Herald* that the McCollom brothers had loaded their last wagon and were ready to go home, but the chute men were not ready and they were delayed. Had they left when the gangway men were ready, all the men felt they would have been killed because they would have been at the spot where the fall occurred.

So how did these men react to being trapped? Edmonds said they all lay down in a wagon to rest and then Fisher played several games of quoits with the youth to keep the boy's spirits up.

All of these men continued to work in or around the mines for the rest of their lives, including Henry Fisher, my great-grandfather. Just a year earlier, his younger brother, George Wesley, had been killed in an accident at the Cameron. Two other brothers would die later in mining accidents: William, in 1902, and Elias, in 1918.

A Great Loss

Here's another with a personal connection. The July 26, 1878 edition of the *Northumberland County Democrat* reported the following:

> On Thursday July 11th a rope broke at one of the slopes at Cameron Colliery, which struck and almost instantly killed George Westly Fisher, cutting his arm clean off and otherwise mutilating him. He was aged about seventeen years and was a son of Mr. Jacob Fisher of Shamokin. His death is a great loss to his father, to whom he was a great help.

Jacob Fisher was my second great-great-grandfather. George Wesley, who was born April 14, 1861 and died in that tragic accident on July 18, 1878, was one of three sons lost to mining accidents. His was not the only family to suffer such devastating losses.

Unfortunate Family

A fatal accident at the Cameron Colliery on Saturday, August 17, 1878, added another chapter to a history of misfortune for one Shamokin family.

The story was reported in the August 23 edition of the *Shamokin Times*. According to the report, Saturday was payday for the Mineral Railroad and Mining Company and employees at the Cameron quit work earlier than normal, most coming out of the mine shortly after noon.

When Samuel Carl and John H. Richards didn't arrive home by that evening, their families inquired at the Mineral offices. It was discovered that the men failed to pick up their pay and hadn't been seen by their fellows. A party was soon formed to search for the men. Among the searchers was Peter Carl, brother of Samuel. Others involved were Charles Henninger and Simon Sober.

Richards and Carl were working as butties in the Deep Slope, in breast No. 74. They were heard to fire a shot between 11 and 12 o'clock. The exploring party first visited the breast in which the men had been working, but they found that the men had gone. The shot was dressed off and the tools carefully placed on top of the coal, as if the men had quit work to come out.

The two were found in the adjoining breast, Carl dead and Richards unconscious. A coroner's jury later surmised that the force of the shot knocked Carl into the manway and in falling he struck Richards, who was below him. Carl was believed to have been killed instantly. Richards suffered a gash on his head and the newspaper reported him still unable to speak on the twenty-third.

Carl, who lived on Commerce Street, was about 28 years old and left a wife and three children. The *Times* noted he belonged to a family that had been "very unfortunate." A brother, Daniel, was killed at the Cameron two years earlier, leaving a wife and two children. Another brother (name unreadable in copy) had his hand crippled by a blast at a mine in St. Clair. Peter, the brother who was involved in the search, was accidentally shot by an elder brother some years earlier, the ball passing through both hands and lodging in his leg. The wound in his leg never properly healed and he lost three fingers. Peter also was burned twice and once had his collarbone fractured in mining accidents. Adding more grief, the mother of the Carl boys had suffered a paralytic stroke two months earlier.

Dark Corner

A woman's curiosity gave residents of Dark Corner, a patch near Centralia, a scare on the night of April 18, 1880.

The incident was reported in the April 29 edition of the *Shamokin Herald* and copied from the April 22 edition of the *Ashland Record*.

Our little village was thrown into a state of excitement on last Sunday evening, between five and six o'clock by a loud crash followed by a cloud of dust raising in the air, in the direction of the Continental Slope Engine House.

Men, women and children began running in the direction of the colliery, supposing that the boilers had exploded and the breaker (which is largely their support) would be consumed by fire.

Upon arriving at the colliery, the real nature of the accident was discovered. The heavy timbers which support the sheaves, upon which the ropes run, at the top of the slope, were lying broken and scattered in every direction. High up, almost on a level with the engine bed, hung a car, partly loaded with coal, and almost totally wrecked.

It was not until much later that the cause of the mishap was discovered. The engineer had gone for his supper, leaving Michael Cleary, the fireman, in charge. Cleary's wife came to visit and he showed her around and explained the workings of the various machines.

At some point, Cleary had to leave the engine house for a short time. In his absence, Mrs. Cleary thought she would try her hand at working the equipment.

> ... inspired by the heroism of modern women, (she) grasped the steam bar of the engine, put on full force of steam, and then fled for her life.
>
> The cars were hanging part way down the slope, and when the ascending one had reached the top it was going at a rapid rate. Mr. Cleary having heard the engine in motion, ran toward the engine house, but had scarcely reached the door when the car was dashed to pieces against the stone bed of the engine. It made a fearful racket, and was heard in Centralia, a distance of over one mile.

The article didn't say what repercussions Mrs. Cleary faced but work at the colliery was suspended for three days while repairs were undertaken.

Burning Mines

People throughout the coal region are familiar with the story of the underground mine fire that has made Centralia, Columbia County, a ghost town.

Despite its reputation, this was not the first unquenchable fire to cause devastation, nor should it be expected to be the last. The *Sunbury American* of November 5, 1880 reported the failure of all attempts to extinguish a fire which had been raging for several weeks in the Keeley Run colliery in Schuylkill County. It was feared this would add another "... to the perpetually burning mines that now exist in the Pennsylvania anthracite region."

The article recounted the history of a fire in the jugular vein, near Coal Castle, Norwegian Township, Schuylkill County, which had been burning since 1835 and was considered the greatest of these fires.

Lewis F. Dougherty opened the vein in 1833. The upper drift of the mine was above water level and a fire was kept burning in a grate at the mouth of the mine in winter to keep the water from freezing in the gutters. One night in 1835 fire from the grate ignited the timbers. The blaze was carried down the air hole to the lower drifts and, by the time it was discovered, proved beyond control.

Two miners entered, intent on recovering their tools. They never came out.

Though it was considered some of the best coal in the region, Dougherty abandoned the mine.

In 1865 John McGinnis put in a new slope to the east and below the water level. "He struck the vein at a place where the coal was so thick that two miners could keep a large breaker supplied. When 400 yards of gangway had been excavated, the heat from the burning Dougherty mine began to bother the miners."

McGinnis attempted to open an air hole, but this failed to alleviate the problem.

> The heat became so great that the men were paid double wages to induce them to work. They worked entirely naked, and were relieved every 10 minutes. Finally the heat became so intense that work was abandoned.
>
> The mine was flooded. After being pumped out men could again work for a few days. The mine was flooded nine times. McGinnis finally failed, and the mine was then abandoned. The fire has been raging in the vein ever since.

This newspaper account of 1880 said millions of dollars of the best quality of coal were consumed by the fire.

> An area of a half mile in every direction has been burned. No vegetation grows on the surface. In places the ground has caved in, forming chasms a hundred feet deep. There is but a thin shell of earth over the pit of fire. At night blue sulphurous flames issue from the crevices in the ground. The stones on the ground are

hot, and snow never rests there. Rain turns to vapor as fast as it falls on the roof of the burning mine.

Noting the danger of walking in the area, the article reported the disappearance of several persons who it was believed had fallen into the mine in the previous 20 years. In fact, it was reported that Dougherty, the original owner, had once sank through the crust to his armpits and was only saved by brave workers who ventured to his assistance.

Gas in the Tunnels

Damp—noxious fumes given off by the mineral—was the cause of many tragedies that occurred in this area during the heyday of anthracite mining. Some types of damp are explosive, while others have a tendency to be poisonous. One such incident involving the latter variety occurred in August 1884 when seven lives were lost in Greenback Colliery.

According to a lengthy report in the August 28 issue of the *Shamokin Herald*, the trouble began when a fire was discovered the previous week at the Buck Ridge Colliery. The two collieries were only a mile and a half apart and in the drifts above the water level the gangways of both had been driven toward one another. Officials planned to cut a hole through a pillar at the face of a gangway, turn the creek into the Greenback slope through the water level, and drown out the fire at Buck Ridge.

A crew of three men began the work Wednesday afternoon, August 20. They were to be relieved at 11:00 that night by another team. For some reason, Dennis Burns, a member of the relief crew, went to work early. He lay down in the boiler house to await his "butties," fell asleep, and did not awaken until long after the others had descended. Having missed his assignment, he went home and, fortunately for him, survived.

Thursday morning as Peter Welker, inside stable boss, was being let down on a truck to feed the mules, the truck passed over what he discovered to be the body of a man. Welker crawled up the slope and by the time he reached the surface was nearly overcome by after-damp forced from the burning slope at Buck Ridge.

The alarm was given and work was begun immediately to build an air trunk from the top of the fan to the mouth of the slope. During the bratticing, 18 men were overcome by the gas and had to be resuscitated. Even after the fan was started, the damp continued to be dangerous. At one point a dog was lowed into the slope to test the air and the animal was overcome, but later revived.

It wasn't until Saturday morning that the last of the bodies was recovered by their brave fellows who put their own lives at risk by laboring amid the poisonous fumes.

Those lost in the tragedy were: William Clark, 33, of Brady, who left a wife and three daughters; William Carroll, 35, Greenback Patch, survived by a wife and six children; Patrick Healy, 35, Brady, who left a wife and seven children; Jonas William Taylor, 24, who had a wife and two children; William Shankweiler, 26, who had a wife and five children; George Beck, 36, a wife and five children; and Robert White, who would have been 15 had he lived until the 10th of the following month.

Culm Explosion

Several people narrowly escaped with their lives and some thought it was the end of the world when a culm bank exploded and fire broke out at Luke Fidler.

The story was reported in the August 2, 1889 edition of the *Shamokin Herald*. Several people narrowly escaped with their lives and many thought it was the end of the world.

At 3 o'clock on the afternoon of July 30, John Bennett was taking a number of loaded dumpers of dirt from the head of the plane to a siding near the end of the bank. Halfway out, he notified George Fabel and Joseph Hayes, two dumpsmen at the end of the bank, of his approach by blowing his whistle. Just as he did so, Bennett saw a black volume of smoke and dirt rise 30 feet over the banks. He assumed a house was on fire. But, on arriving at the siding, the men told him the bank exploded.

Hayes and Fabel had just dumped two wagons of dirt on a side pitch. At that point the bank was 150 feet high and the base fronted on the Mount Carmel Pike. Fifty feet from the base and just off the pike stood a single frame house, owned by the Mineral Mining Company and occupied by the family of John Boney.

After the dirt was unloaded, two wagons of rock were run out onto the track. As one was about to be unloaded, Hayes looked down the bank and was amazed to see tongues of fire and black smoke issue from the dirt. "My God, what's the matter?" he cried. But his companion, who had his back turned, pulled the pin and released another cascade of rock. When the rock struck the dirt, the edge of the bank nearest the rails began sliding.

The rocks and dirt struck the center of the flames and there was an explosion. "As if hurled from a battery of Krupp guns, a thousand balls of red hot rock went high up in the air, while a river of fire ran down the bank like lightning into Boney's yard," the *Herald* reported.

Hayes saw a woman picking coal at the bottom in a direct line of the course the flaming stream of fire took. It was Mrs. Boney and with her was her 4-year-old son, James. Hayes shouted to alert her. He saw her run, then a cloud of smoke and dirt obscured her from his sight.

The fiery stream rushed off the bank and ran down her yard in a compact body estimated at three feet deep. Mrs. Boney made it out to the road but, somehow, was separated from her child and didn't know what had become of him. She feared the fire would ignite the house but, fortunately, a recent heavy rain had saturated the siding and it did not catch. As she watched, another volume of dirt slid down the yard and extinguished the fire. When she entered the house she found that her son had made it inside and was huddled with his 75-year-old grandmother and several other children in the kitchen. Trees in the yard had been scorched and a dog caught in the track of the fire was cremated.

The *Herald* reported that smoke hid the surroundings for a mile around and people living in Springfield and Boydtown said they thought it was the end of the world.

In seeking a cause for the conflagration it was found that dirt had been dumped off the east side of the plane for a dozen years. Some five years previous to the blast, people picking coal had built a fire at the base to warm themselves. The flame ignited the coal and the bank had been burning from the bottom up until that spring when flames appeared on top the north side. Four months earlier jigs were put in the breaker to clean coal and the dirt became wet, a dumper often being half filled with water when it was taken to the bank.

Authorities surmised that a large hole was eaten in the bank where gas accumulated and was kept in by the wet dirt, which finally became dried from the heat, admitted air, and resulted in the explosion.

The only similar event reported in the area was at the Reppalier Colliery at Ashland 20 years earlier when the town was completely inundated by flying dirt and fire.

That Sinking Feeling

Though the cause was uncertain, residents of Ashland were understandably concerned when the ground began sinking beneath their feet in some sections of the community in the fall of 1889.

The situation was reported in the November 15, 1889 edition of the *Shamokin Herald* and several theories were advanced to explain the problem. The alleged explanations may have been of little comfort to those whose property was affected. According to the newspaper, the trouble was first reported about a week earlier.

"Since that time the ground has been sinking or settling west of Twelfth Street, and although various causes are attributed to this strange state of affairs no correct or positive solution to the matter has as yet been advanced."

Numerous residents came forth with complaints. A Mrs. Klock said the pavement in front of her residence between Fourteenth and Fifteenth streets had sunk several inches. The foundation walls of B. M. Slobig's brick home gradually were giving way, and from the pavement one could see into his cellar through an opening of about two inches.

Mrs. H. Hanburger said her building had sunk to such an extent that she could not shut her doors easily. Timothy Kinney claimed there was an opening of three inches in the floor of his cellar and the walls had sunk several inches. Nick Orth reported that his barber shop was badly damaged.

One of the most extreme reports had to do with the new building of the Washington Fire Company.

What was a short time ago a costly structure is now a dilapidated building. A few weeks ago was first noticed signs of the building sinking, since which time much damaged has been done. The building seems to be spreading apart and from top to bottom there is evidence of that fact.

One theory was that the sinking was caused by the settling of the old Wadleigh and Bancroft tunnels, which ran below the town. However, it was pointed out that those workings did not extend as far as the places where the trouble occurred.

One mining authority suggested it might be caused by an underground strata of clay washing out as a result of recent heavy rains. He felt there might still be some slight sinking but did not believe it would prove to be anything serious.

Cameron Fire

Passage of time has dimmed memories of another fire that caused economic distress in Shamokin.

That fire began February 25, 1890 deep within the tunnels of Cameron Colliery. The blaze defied all efforts to extinguish it and took until mid-April for authorities to come up with a plan that finally succeeded. The disaster already posed a hard blow to the community since, at the time, the colliery gave employment to some 1,400 men and boys.

Other area collieries experienced a slump over the winter due to contract issues and the economic situation might have been worse had they not resumed work in April.

On April 11, the *Shamokin Herald* announced the resumption of work at the Henry Clay and also reported that a decision had been reached to flood the Cameron in an effort to put out the fire.

> Tomorrow morning workmen will be employed in digging a ditch to turn the waters of Shamokin Creek into the mine. The workings up to the water level can be flooded in three or four days, but this would cause an immense damage to the mine. By taking more time this would be lessened. It is estimated that it will take six months to pump the water out, and, it may be, a[n] equal length of time to place the colliery in working order.

Subsequently, the *Herald* reported that large crowds turned out, from early morning till night, to observe the project. "The creek has been dammed up just above the fan house and a ditch carries the contents of the stream through the air duct to the subterranean passages below."

While the flooding and pumping out of the mine continued other miners were put to work developing veins above the water level. It was estimated that 400 wagons a day could be taken from these workings.

It was not until September 5 that the *Herald* reported that the work of pumping water out of the Cameron was complete.

The reopening of the Cameron after that devastating fire was occasion for celebration as reported in the September 12, 1890 edition of the *Shamokin Herald*.

The celebration began on Saturday, September 6, with a parade through the community, followed by a picnic at Lot's Grove. The parade proceeded from the offices of the colliery, led by William Hodge, chief marshal; Harry Morgan and Edward Brennan, outside and inside foremen; an old gray mule and cart bearing three cranks of the colliery; the Shamokin Band; 75 miners; and a float containing a boiler and pump.

An estimated 400 persons attended the picnic and were addressed by Henry F. Yost, tip man at the colliery.

He began with the history of the memorable evening, the 26th of February, when the shrill sound of the Cameron whistles gave the alarm of fire and men, women and children rushed to the colliery, intensely excited. They learned that the fire was in the mine at the bottom of slope No. 1 vein, No. 9 gangway. He described the hurry and flurry to see that the workmen were all safe and to bring out the mules, if possible.

Yost went on to describe the lengthy fight, which went on till the end of March when it became apparent that the only way to save the valuable property was to flood it and drown out the raging inferno of fire. After extinguishing the fire, several more months were needed to pump out the water so work could resume.

"Think of it," Yost told the crowd, "an estimated one million gallons of water were taken out in less than four months, without injuring a man or doing any damage to the hoisting machinery, which was kept running continually from the beginning."

A sidebar to the article said about 200 wagon loads of dirt, mostly sand from the bottom of Shamokin Creek, was washed into the mine during the flooding. It was noted that anthracite trade was improving and officials estimated an additional 200 miners would be given work in the coming weeks.

In addition to speeches, food, and drink the picnic continued until dusk and included several running matches, a baseball game, cake walks, and music by Shamokin Band, which gave its services throughout the day without charge.

Tornado Damage

Though its football team is known as the Red Tornadoes, Mount Carmel generally has been spared the ravages of killer storms of the same name because of its geographical position, sheltered by surrounding mountains.

But a tornado was blamed for demolishing a breaker and killing seven men on June 26, 1891 less than a mile from the borough limits.

According to contemporary newspaper accounts, the Patterson Coal Company's breaker was crushed by a tornado that struck just after 3 p.m.

At the time the wind struck the colliery it was in full operation. Suddenly there was a crash and the huge structure swayed to and fro for a moment and then fell to the ground, a mass of ruins. When the crash came many of the employees rushed from the breaker, panic stricken, while others who were less fortunate were caught in the flying timbers and crushed to death.

Killed were J. N. Blossom, 40, of Hawley; B. Dodson, 35, Shickshinney; Walter Robert, 27, and William Lodge, 24, both of Luzerne; and three others identified only as Italians. Five other persons were injured, two seriously.

Lodge, Roberts, and two of the unidentified men were slaters, engaged in roofing the breaker at the time of the storm. Blossom and Dodson were carpenters and were killed while at work inside the structure.

After the accident occurred the wildest excitement followed, and the employees as well the people living near by flocked to the scene of disaster and aided those who were fortunate enough to escape in removing the dead and injured from the wrecked breaker.

A passenger on the Philadelphia and Reading express train, which passed through the storm, told a reporter,

When the train reached Locust Summit on its way to Philadelphia I saw the storm approaching from the southwest. We had not gone far when it struck the train. A panic followed and it was feared that the entire train would be hurled from the track. Trees were uprooted on either side and the noise produced by the

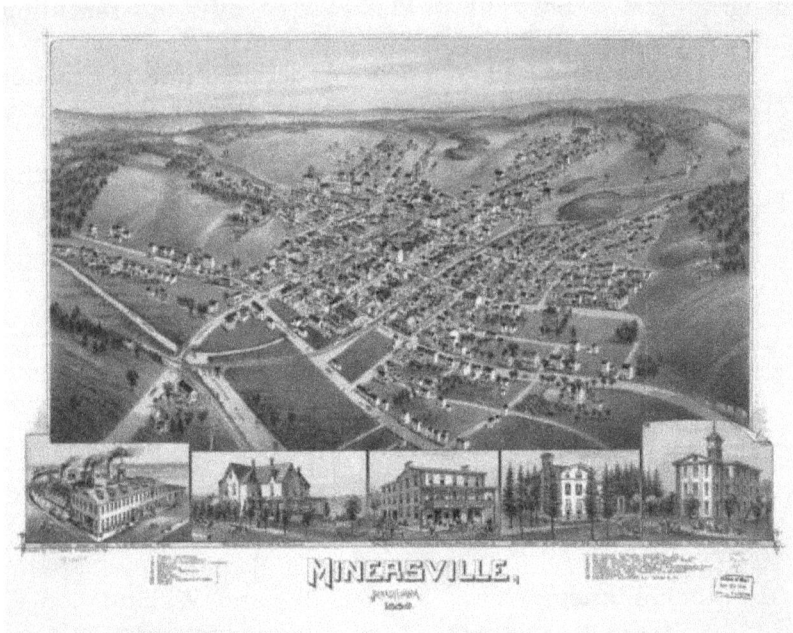

Minersville, 1889.

rushing wind reminded me of the roaring of musketry. The storm seemed to increase in violence every moment until the train reached Gordon, some miles east, when it abated.

Drowned in the Tunnels

Eleven lives were lost April 21, 1892, when water burst through the face of a breast at the Lytle coal company's mine near Minersville. A not unusual incident in our mining history, but there was a Shamokin and an ethnic angle to this tragedy.

The water had been imprisoned in an older working and completely inundated the Lytle works. According to a report in the April 22 edition of the *Shamokin Herald*, 12 men were imprisoned by the rush of water and only one escaped. William Bell of Jonestown, Schuylkill County, reached an elevated point and was rescued later that night.

The dead were identified as Thomas Buggy, Black Heath; James Dolbin, Forestville; John H. Zerbey,

Llewellyn; and eight Italians, all from Shamokin: Albert Sebella, Frank Vegetta, Natsi Perena, Peter Olivetti, Peter Maketto, Joe Fietta, Vincent Vercuro, and Dominick Uquilla.

It was found later that the water was imprisoned in the Little Diamond gangway, belonging to the old McDonald workings, which had been abandoned years earlier. The Lytle colliery at Primrose, about a mile west of Minersville, was a new plant and had not yet erected a breaker. The operation was controlled by a Scranton syndicate headed by John H. and James P. Hosia. Two tunnels were being driven by the Italians and they were at the lowest level of the mine when the flood bore down upon them.

Sebella, who the newspaper article identified as "... one of the best rockmen in the country," recruited workers under contract for mines all over the region. It was reported that he was not working at the mine but had joined his men earlier in the week to see how they were getting on at the Primrose project.

Ironically, the newspaper pointed out, he had been the intended victim of a murder some years earlier, escaping when Pietro Seccara shot another man who resembled him. Seccara was sentenced to Eastern Penitentiary but slit his own throat and died in custody.

Fall of Coal

Falling coal or rock was another hazard daily faced by miners. The Friday, May 19, 1893 edition of the *Shamokin Herald* reported the death of one man and serious injuries to three others in such accidents at two separate mines.

Michael Dabota was instantly killed by a fall of coal at Big Mountain while working in a breast. Dabota reportedly heard the top crack but was unable to get away in time. A large piece struck him on the back and head. The victim was married and the father of three children. Another miner narrowly escaped being struck by the same fall.

A fall of top rock injured three other men at the Luke Fidler. The victims, all residents of Springfield, were identified as Frank Burzicki, Paul Bogdan, and Anthony

Zackiewicz. It was the latter's first day working in the mines.

The newspaper said the three were engaged in setting timber at the face and would have been going home in a short while. Suddenly a sharp crack resounded, warning them of an impending fall. Bogdan, who stood directly under the point where the report emanated, shouted for his companions to run. Before he could move, the fall occurred, completely covering him. Some of the debris caught the other men, who were knocked down. Once they recovered, Burzicki and Zackiewicz shouted for help and commenced digging out Bogdan who was beneath a large pile of rock and dirt.

Bogdan suffered back injuries. Burzicki and Zackiewicz also suffered cuts and bruises. Dr. Frank Meek, attending physician, expressed hope that all would recover. Based on the 1900 census, all three victims survived.

Cameron Deaths

The deaths of two men at the Cameron Colliery in Shamokin were reported in the Friday, June 15, 1893 edition of the *Shamokin Herald*.

Jesse Watkins, the 18-year-old son of Alexander Watkins, a Reading railroad engineer residing at 122 North Pearl Street, was killed when he was struck by a rush of coal in a chute.

The youth was employed as a starter in the East drift. Fellow workers recalled later that he came to work in the morning in high spirits, laughing and chatting with others.

The miners lost sight of him later in the day but no one was concerned because a starter's duties often isolated them for hours at a time. About 4:30 p.m. inquiries began as to the youth's whereabouts. When John Thomas, one of the bosses, was alerted, he began investigating.

A chute was found jammed with coal. John Thomas summoned Patrick Curry, Michael O'Brien, and George Thomas. A string of wagons was run in the gangway and the men started to empty the chute. The sixth wagon was partly loaded before they discovered the body of the boy.

The other accident involved a young man identified as Clarence Henry of Dewart Street.

Henry was shoveling coal from between pulleys at the bottom of a slope. Two wagons were hoisted up the slope and, as they neared the top, the hind wagon jumped the track, became unlocked, and sped down the steep incline.

Henry evidently didn't hear or see the wagon in time to get away. It struck him and knocked him forty feet away. The wagon followed and stopped directly atop the body of the unfortunate man. The bottom boss had stepped into the safety hole and called to Henry. Getting no answer, he feared the worst and called for men to investigate.

Henry was still alive when found, but expired soon after.

Luke Fidler Fire

Disobedience of a standing order was blamed for a disastrous fire that killed five persons in the fall of 1894 at the Luke Fidler Colliery.

The fire is believed to have started because carpenters working in a shaft used naked lamps rather than lanterns, as was the rule. According to a report in the October 12, 1894 edition of the *Northumberland Public Press*, Irwin Buffington and other carpenters were caulking holes in the side of a brattice, which connected the shaft with an air passage.

Detecting a leak, Buffington placed his lamp to the draught and the flame immediately caught the boards, which were saturated with oil, and was taken into the air chamber. Realizing the awful consequence of his act, the man at once started for the bottom of the shaft to notify the workmen employed there of their danger, his companions, in the meantime, rushing up the shaft to safety.

Though he succeeded in saving some lives, Buffington lost his own because he paused to exchange his rubber boots for shoes. The delay resulted in him being overcome by smoke within 30 feet of safety. The other dead were identified as George Brown, miner; Michael Buzofskie, laborer; Anthony Cobert, driver boy; and John Glerze, laborer.

Michael Golden, one of the inside officials, was at the bottom of the shaft when the alarm was given and he at once notified the men working in No. 3 slope, while John Dunmore performed a like duty for those employed in No. 2 slope. Golden told the men of an opening by which it was possible to reach a new shaft, and leading the way for the seventy men employed in this portion of the mine Golden made for the passage, which was safely reached, although it was nearly filled with smoke.

The iron bucket used to hoist the men holds about six persons. This was quickly filled and in response to the frantic signal given by those below the engineer began to hoist. Nearly 10 trips had been made when it was discovered that a number were missing, among them David Edmonds and Harry Evans.

These two had been forced back by heavy smoke. They then proceeded to the east and were halfway to safety when Evans, a young boy, gave out. Edmunds picked him up and carried the lad until they reached the open air.

Damage from the fire was estimated at $700,000 and it was expected that the thousand men employed at the mine would be idled for months while it was flooded with water to quench the flames.

Another Explosion

An explosion killed two miners and injured more than a dozen in the Susquehanna Coal Company's Scott Shaft about four miles from Shamokin on June 7, 1913. The explosion occurred in the second lift of a slope, almost a mile below ground, and ignited a fire in the shaft.

Early reports indicated that other men were trapped below.

John Weir, inside superintendent, organized a rescuing party and sent them below. Because of the danger of poisonous fumes, the most advanced rescuers wore oxygen helmets. Within an hour of the accident two dead and 14 injured miners were brought to the surface. The dead were identified as George Soduskie and Steve Wargen, both of Mount Carmel. Two of the injured men were reported to be in serious condition.

Most of the miners who were employed at the shaft lived in Kulpmont and in what one newspaper report called "an incredibly short space of time" an estimated 1,000 people had gathered at the site, "... many of the women weeping and wringing their hands in despair as they learned their husbands were among those in the burning slope."

William Reinhart, general superintendent, and his assistant, Richard Holland, gathered experienced first aid personnel from various company collieries and dispatched them by automobile with bundles of blankets to the scene of the accident. Physicians were also summoned. As soon as the rescued miners were brought to the surface they were encased in oiled clothes and blankets and taken by ambulance to the miners' hospitals at Tharptown and Fountain Springs.

After several more hours, the rescuing party came upon a group of 20 miners in the burning shaft. These men were unhurt and they were quickly taken to the surface and reunited with their families. No others were believed to be in the mine.

LABOR WOES
4.
No Unions Wanted

Despite claims of support for the consumer and sympathy for the miner, reading early newspapers shows that a disproportionate number in the coal region were vehemently anti-union and pro-operator. An exception was the *Shenandoah Herald,* where Thomas J. Foster from the start was sympathetic to the Workingmen's Benevolent Association, the first of the coal unions.

This anti-union attitude may have had as much to do with economics as with provincialism. After all, the majority of their revenue came from the operators. There was also a genuine desire for stability and growth in their communities, which would be disposed against the violence resulting as tempers flared during a strike.

Benjamin Bannan, editor of the *Miners' Journal* in Pottsville, conceded in 1849 that miners had a right to strike if it went no further than "... an honest, prudent effort to better their conditions." But he strongly opposed having a committee speak for the miners. "It would be better to let all our Collieries rot and our region become wilderness than such tyranny should be engrafted on the business of this region by a few restless spirits."

Dr. J. J. John also cautioned against strikes in the Thursday, August 24, 1865 edition of the *Shamokin Herald,* noting that "they don't pay. Men lose more than they gain by them."

"We are assured by operators whose word can be relied upon," he wrote, "that the present price of coal will not warrant an increased price for labor, and if the men demand it they must close their works."

He urged instead, "When you think wages are not high enough, let there be a fair and square appeal to your employer, and if he can grant it he will do so if he is an honest man. If he can't, he will say so, and then it is better to go on at the old rates than 'strike' and be idle for weeks."

John contended that it was in the best interest of both the operator and the laborer to have the work continue without interruption and they should be united in desiring to see each weekly shipment of coal an increase over the year before.

We have now increased facilities for shipment. We have increased capital. We have the wealth within our mountains. All we now need to secure prosperity for the town and region is industry, energy and unanimity. Let us have no stagnation by strikes; no division of strife between capital and labor, and success and growth are sure.

Everybody Lies

In the case of nearly every labor agitation, reports make it clear that all parties were guilty of a certain amount of fact twisting to make their case. Sometimes it's necessary to look for evidence outside the coal regions to assess the reality of the situation.

In the wake of a trade deadlock in 1871, the *Public Ledger* of Philadelphia noted on February 27:

... the coal operators and the coal carrying companies have united in defence of their respective interests in the trade, as against what they allege to be the damaging effect of the 'strikes' of the miners and workmen. The result of the differences up to this time is a dead lock in the trade.

Coal production has almost entirely ceased, and, in the face of the gradual wasting away of the limited stocks of coal on hand, the retailers, with the aid of the more sensational writers of the press, are running the prices of coal up on consumers largely, and, as we are constrained to believe, unnecessarily.

The best informed in the trade, and those who have had the most to do in adjusting differences, are sanguine in the opinion that resumption of work at the mines will not be many days delayed, and that the stocks of coal at the great centres are abundant, especially for domestic uses, until trade is resumed.

In the same article, the *Ledger* accused the unions of also being adroit when it came to facts on the wage issue, which was a sticking point in the dispute. Operators wanted the minimum basis for adjustment of wages set at $2 per ton while the unions were demanding $2.50.

The President of one of the associations has made a statement in detail on this point. This, however, is a question which has two sides, as we will show from reliable figures taken from the pay roll of one of the largest firms of operators in the coal trade. To show the specious character of the official paper alluded to, and to correct the misapprehension of the press and the public on this matter it is but necessary to state that the prices are set forth as the weekly wages, or the average full wages of a miner, when the fact is that hardly one miner in fifty works by the day or week, the work of mining coal being virtually all done by contract or piece-work, at which the wages earned are twice or thrice the price fixed as a standard by which to pay for the small amount of work done by miners at day's work.

The *Ledger* was wrong in believing that the matter would be settled in days. It dragged on until April when Governor John W. Geary forced both sides into arbitration. By that time, warmer weather had eased fears of fuel shortages and nearly everyone was tired of the wrangling.

Meanwhile, Franklin B. Gowen, newly elected president of the Philadelphia & Reading Railroad, was busily buying up coal lands. Many smaller operators were in serious financial straits, giving Gowen a great deal of leverage to acquire an expanding domain. With the Reading as the dominant carrier, other operators as well as the miners were between the proverbial rock and a hard place.

The next step in Gowen's plan was to blame future labor agitations on that terrorist organization, the Molly Maguires.

Long Strike

During the so-called "Long Strike" of 1875, a group of striking miners, predominately from Luzerne County, marched on Schuylkill County, intent on shutting down operations there. National Guard troops from Shamokin, Locust Gap, St. Clair, and Girardville were called in to assist police in restoring order.

The *Shamokin Herald* of Thursday, June 10, 1875, carried a long report on what transpired, quoting from other newspapers in the area. There are varying opinions on whether the incident was instigated by the Mollie Maguires and some of the reports may be biased.

From the *Tamaqua Courier*:

Our town was thrown into a fever of excitement on Thursday afternoon last by a report that a large body of miners had marched during the night, from Luzerne County to Mahanoy City, for the purpose of stopping the miners from working at Lentz & Bowman's colliery, and that the military had been called out. The news was confirmed soon after by the appearance of the military on their way to Mahanoy City. Subsequently we learned that the Luzerne miners, accompanied by others from neighboring 'patches' of Mahanoy City, had stopped work at the places known as N. Mahanoy, Staffordshire, Primrose, Beaver Run and Hartford collieries.

From the *Pottsville Miner's Journal*:

... several hundred rioters were gathered at the Forrester colliery, operated by King, Tyler & Co., and forced the men to quit work. Sheriff Werner, who had been called from Shenandoah, summoned a posse of 20 or 30 of the citizens and police, armed with revolvers and proceeded to the spot, accompanied by a crowd of men. He ordered the rioters to disperse and was going to read the Riot Act, but one turbulent fellow precipitated matters and the rioters opened fire on the Sheriff and party, firing in all about 100 shots.

One officer was shot in the ankle, another struck on the head by a stone, and two others were hurt. It was reported that eight of the rioters were shot, at least one seriously.

After the encounter with the sheriff, the rioters formed and boldly marched through town, down Centre street, towards St. Nicholas, where they separated and probably took to the hills. They are said to have been led by a fellow from Girardville. Stores and houses were closed and a rush was made to the hardware store for firearms.

Following the arrival of the military, things apparently quieted down, for the *Pottsville Republican* reported: "The suspended collieries will all go to work in the morning. The men from the Lehigh region robbed the farmers of Rush Township last night, taking whatever they could lay hands on."

Clergy Oppose Strike

While claiming to sympathize with the plight of the miner, clergy of Shamokin spoke out against a proposed strike in the anthracite coal region in the September 9, 1900 edition of the *Philadelphia Inquirer*.

The newspaper had solicited and published comments from five prominent clergy of the community. Those commenting were Rev. D. S. Monroe, pastor, First Methodist Episcopal Church; Rev. C. B. Schneder, pastor, Reformed Church; Rev. Joseph Koch, pastor, St. Edward's Catholic Church; Rev. W. E. Fischer, pastor, Trinity Lutheran Church; and Rev. J. W. Gilland, pastor, Presbyterian Church.

Admitting he was "not much acquainted with the situation of miners in the region," Monroe argued that strikes were generally brought on "... by leaders who mislead miners."

He said:

I am a friend of the workingman, but I have found in the soft coal region where I lived many years that strikes are seldom successful. I have met American and English speaking miners in Shamokin and every one is opposed to a strike. They claim they get along quite well and receive good raises.

Schneder seemed a bit more concerned for the welfare of the miner, citing a fear that the cost of a strike would be more than improved conditions sought, "... even if the operator were to concede everything." Expressing hope that a strike might be averted, he added that he heartily favored any other measures that might improve conditions for miners.

Father Koch said he and other priests of Shamokin and vicinity were advising mining men of their congregations to avoid a strike.

I am opposed to a strike for the reason that past experiences have taught bitter lessons to the miners of this region. When a committee of the union men called upon me last Saturday they remarked that their only grievance was for 20 per cent of a raise. I do not look at the strike, but its consequences. What will become of the wives and children of the idle men who are not prepared to drop their tools?

Reverend Fischer also commented on the consequences of a strike.

The labor problem is worldwide. Nine-tenths of the race are laborers. With a proper adjustment of society every laboring man may be happy and contented. His condition is vastly improved today as compared with the past.

His right to organize against every form of injustice is not disputed. Public sentiment must be further strengthened to enforce arbitration. There must be patience and manly conduct on the part of the laborer if he would secure enlarged rights.

Reverend Gilland said:

> I am willing to do or say anything consistent or reasonable to avert such an untoward calamity as a strike would inflict upon our community." All my training and associations naturally make me sympathize with the laboring man. I have been a laborer myself, and all my early experiences were those of a workingman.
>
> But I could not appreciate nor could I sympathize with laboring men who are so easily duped and so unreasonably led as our laboring men are now being advised and persuaded by the irresponsible agitators who have come into our region at this time.

Previously, an article in the September 1, 1900 edition of the *Inquirer* claimed that 75 percent of men in the Shamokin District were opposed to the proposed strike.

However, it should be noted that the statement came from individual operators and representatives of the various coal companies of the region. The article said the district employed 20,000 men and boys and embraced territory from Lykens, Dauphin County; Shamokin, Northumberland County; to Ashland, Schuylkill County, and total shipment for the previous year was nearly six million tons. Shamokin was cited as the heart of the district.

> Since the present strike talk, owing to operators and representatives of coal companies not meeting representatives of the United Mine Workers at Hazleton, a careful poll of the Shamokin District men shows that 75 percent of the working men are adverse to obeying orders to strike. Their principal grievance is the non-observance of the semi-monthly pay law.

The company representatives said that if the miners had grievances they were willing to treat them individually but would not tolerate Western labor leaders coming into the country and dictating terms.

The operators will not meet the United Mine Workers as a body. If a strike must come, the quicker it is fought out so much the better it will be for all concerned and, realizing that the mass of our men do not want to cease work, it would seem that the strike, once called, will, if it materializes, be of an abortive nature.

Strike of 1902

"Terror Rules in the Coal Region" screamed a headline in the August 1, 1902 edition of the *Sunbury American*.

The article highlighted spreading violence in the wake of the anthracite coal strike launched on May 12 by the United Mine Workers of America (UMWA). Miners across the region went on strike seeking higher wages, a shorter workday and recognition of the union. The newspaper cited a "reign of terror" at collieries in Shamokin, Mount Carmel, and Shenandoah against non-union members desiring to work.

The pent-up feeling of anger against non-union men which burst out at Shenandoah Monday (July 28) in which one man was shot by strikers and so badly wounded that chances are against his recovery, is gaining in violence and is rapidly spreading throughout the entire region.

It was reported that an attack was made by strikers against non-union men on their way home from work on Tuesday, July 29, 1902 in Shamokin.

The trouble occurred at the Henry Clay and Cameron collieries and it is likely that more trouble will follow at both these places.

At the Cameron colliery a large crowd of men, women and boys congregated on a bridge close by and when the non union men passed them on their way home from work they were hooted, jeered and pelted with stones in such a manner that they were forced to flee for safety.

Ten Williamstown miners were arrested in September 1902 for their participation in a strike disturbance in Lykens.

The strikers received strong support in the community.

A story in the September 26 issue of the *Sunbury American* said the men were taken to Harrisburg for a hearing as a result of their alleged involvement in marching and stoning of houses. Officers armed with warrants arrived in the town, accusing the men of disorderly conduct under a strike act of 1895. Charges were brought by Hood McKay, superintendent of the Lykens Valley Coal Company.

The action spurred "great excitement," resulting in another march by strikers and a walkout by girls employed in two local textile mills. The newspaper said the arresting officers were hooted and jeered.

It was reported that the scene rivaled an incident two years earlier when "... miners, alarmed by the spread of the strike sentiment, laid down their tools and joined the strikers of Lykens and Brookside."

Arrested were James Burns, Tony Greiner, Will Kenker, Joe Plunket, John Rich, Charles Radebush, A. Bretz, Claude Reichert, James Finley, and Will Solladay. Burns, a former policeman, and Plunkett were fined $10 plus costs. Briner, Bretz, Finlay, and Radebush paid fines of $5 each, plus costs. The others were fined $1 each, plus costs.

After the prisoners had been started for Harrisburg the strikers got out the Williamstown Cornet Band and paraded the streets. Members of other unions joined them and the houses of workers and non-union men were hooted. The parading lasted until night and after dark there was continuous blowing of tin horns and battering of powder cans by boys and girls.

The girls employed by the Diamond Knitting Mills company and of the Durbin Hosiery Mill, of Williamstown, struck about noon on the charge that there were non-union girls and girls whose families were non-union working in the mills. They walked out in a body and joined the paraders.

On Sunday, September 28, 1902, the *Sunbury American* reported that, "A large mob of strikers went to the colliery office of T.M. Righter & Company and stormed the building, doing great damage." According to the report, they broke into the office and destroyed furniture, books, and records.

The following day,

> ... the rioting continued and a street car running from Mt. Carmel to Green Ridge, with men on board going to work at the Richards colliery, was held up and stoned. Three workmen on board, John Rafferty, John Penman and Henry Rhoads, were pulled from the car and severely beaten.

County Sheriff Samuel Deitrick was summoned to the scene and swore in as deputies Henry Bickle, Harry Grefsgar, H. O. Dunkleberger, and James Berryman, all mine workers. When they reached the Righter Colliery, they discovered that the strikers had dynamited the steam column pipes and fled.

The strikers marched to Dooleyville and then to Green Ridge. There, an estimated 300 strikers met the miners' train, which transported workers from Shamokin to Green Ridge. A. J. Brittain and a squad of six special officers kept the strikers at gunpoint from entering the train. Brittain ordered the engineer to make for Mount Carmel. As they departed, strikers pelted the train with stones and fired shots into the cars.

"When the train arrived at the Mt. Carmel passenger station those who were on the train made their way to Alaska and went back to Shamokin on the Reading road."

The report continued:

> Monday evening a mob of 2,000 went to the Righter colliery in Mt. Carmel, where the deputies had been placed by the sheriff, and overpowered the deputies, taking possession of the colliery for the second time during the past twenty four hours. Although Sheriff Deitrick did his utmost to protect property and quiet

143

the strikers, he soon realized that the situation was beyond his control.

In response to his call for help, eight companies of the Fourth Regiment, Pennsylvania National Guard were sent in to guard the collieries.

But it wasn't the violence alone that brought the federal government in as a neutral arbitrator for the first time in a labor situation. The strike posed the serious threat of shutting down the winter fuel supply of the nation's major cities. President Theodore Roosevelt interceded and established a fact-finding commission that suspended the strike on October 23 after 163 days.

John Mitchell, president of the UMWA, had proposed a similar solution earlier but was rebuffed by George Baer, president of the Philadelphia and Reading, the industry's leading employer.

Roosevelt's commission toured the coal region in October and set about interviewing witnesses for the industry, the miners, and the non-union workers. Though they eventually concluded that the miners were only partly justified in their claims, their decision split the difference between the two sides. The miners received a 10 percent wage increase rather than the 20 percent they sought and a nine-hour day rather than the requested eight-hour day. While the mine owners still refused to recognize the union they were compelled to accept an arbitration board as a means to settle future labor disputes.

Mitchell called it a victory for the workingmen. Baer sourly remarked, "These men don't suffer. Why, hell, most of them don't even speak English."

CHANGE IS INEVITABLE
5.
The Boom Is Over

Nothing lasts forever. That's as true of an industry as it is of anything else. Coal was the economic foundation for the anthracite region for a good part of two centuries.

Despite another round of crippling nationwide strikes in 1922 and 1925, the 1920s were boom years for the bigger collieries in Northumberland and Schuylkill counties. The hammer fell with the depression that began in 1929. Even the largest were forced into lengthy shutdowns by the lack of revenue in this trying period.

For instance, the Cameron, Shamokin's biggest, which achieved its peak years as a star operation of the Susquehanna Coal Company, shut down in 1929 and did not resume work for 18 months. In 1931 Susquehanna leased the property to the Stevens Coal Company. Susquehanna resumed control in 1940, changing the name of the colliery to Glen Burn.

Despite increasing competition from gas, oil, and electricity, coal experienced another period of prosperity during World War II. But by the 1950s it was clear its position as fuel of choice was over.

I clearly remember as a boy seeing throngs of miners pouring like a stream, their faces blackened, shoulders slumped in weariness, boots shuffling along the paving as they ended their shifts at the Glen Burn. By the time I reached high school their numbers had dwindled; many were unemployed and others were leaving to accept jobs in other states.

U.S. Department of Labor statistics reveal that mine production declined from a peak of 100 million tons in 1917 to 46 million tons in 1950. And by that time nearly a third of the coal being mined came from surface operations or reprocessing of culm banks.

Heavy coal train getting underway from Shamokin in 1913 eastbound for Mahanoy Plane where its cars would be lifted over Broad Mountain. The last engine in this triple-headed consist of pushers was probably added on when the original pair could not move the train. Usually the wooden caboose was hung on the very end because of the danger of it being crushed by one of the powerful Consolidations in the event suddenly stopped. (caption info and photo courtesy The Reading Railroad: History of a Coal Age Empire by James L. Holten)

Timber Problems

Though it may not be immediately apparent to the casual observer, the mining of coal required a considerable amount of timber. This was not a problem in the early days of the industry since the mountains and valleys of the anthracite region were heavily forested and provided an ample supply.

In addition to ordinary building needs, it was common practice to support the roof and sides of mine tunnels with timbers joined close together and sometimes lined by sticks placed behind and over them in a system known as "lagging." Because of the pressure of the earth above them and the constant seepage of water, which rotted the wood, these supports had to be regularly replaced.

Because there was so much forest around them, this was not a problem in the early years. But, by the beginning of the 20th century, Pennsylvania's timber supply was being depleted and importing it from outside the area became a worrisome expense for the operators.

This concern was noted in an article in the December 11, 1923 edition of the *Sunbury American,* quoting a report by Harry E. Tufft, a mining engineer with the U.S. Bureau of Mines.

Tufft reported that the Pennsylvania anthracite region was the largest user of mine timber in any mining district in the United States, with an annual consumption exceeding 100 million cubic feet. He said the average cost of round mine timber had increased from 6.6 cents a cubic foot in 1905 to 27.5 cents a cubic foot delivered to the mine. "Of the present cost, 57.3 per cent," the report said, "represents freight charges."

> Twenty or twenty-five years ago the best grades of white and red oak, chestnut and pitch timber could be obtained locally and the major part of the timber used was hardwoods. The soft woods used were mainly yellow pine with the remainder hemlock and spruce. At that time much of the yellow pine was shipped from the South, according to Mr. Tufft, although most of the other timber was obtained in Pennsylvania.
>
> At present, he declared, perhaps 75 per cent, or more of the timber used in the anthracite region is soft wood, such as loblolly pine and second growth yellow pine, largely shipped from the South.

Tufft pointed out that some operators had gone to the extreme of having trial shipments of Douglas fir brought by ships from Oregon through the Panama Canal to compare quality and costs with that available from the South.

The engineer urged operators to reduce their timber outlay by carefully studying needs and adopting policies to result in better selection of timber for use and to peel, season, and treat with preservatives to extend the life of that put into use.

Bootlegging

During the Depression, many collieries were forced to shut down. Though it was hoped that this would be a temporary measure, many of those operations never worked again. Unemployment compensation programs were still a thing of the future and many miners found themselves and their families in desperate straits. By 1932, an estimated 16,000 miners in Schuylkill County were out of work. The situation was similar in Northumberland County and the miners were not alone in seeking work. Other industries had also put workers on the streets.

It was a traditional practice throughout the coal region for families to pick coal from the refuse discarded by the breakers for their own use as fuel. This had seldom been a concern to the big companies. Now, suddenly, unemployed men began expanding on this practice by sneaking onto company grounds and sinking holes to mine coal.

The miners didn't view their action as illegal or immoral. It was a matter of survival. If the operators weren't going to mine the coal, they saw no legitimate reason why they shouldn't. And this attitude was supported by many civic and religious leaders in the communities. In fact, one priest, Father Weaver of Mount Carmel, remarked, "Coal bootlegging has no bad moral effect on the people. It keeps them from starving."

Initially men mined a little coal for their own use or to sell to neighbors. Eventually the illegal mining expanded to the point where tons of fuel were being trucked for sale in Philadelphia, Baltimore, and other distant points. One report indicated that 3,500 men and boys were engaged in this illegal trade in Shamokin by the mid 1930s. Similar numbers were noted for other communities in Northumberland and Schuylkill counties. Obviously, the coal companies weren't going to stand idly by and allow this loss.

As they had been in the previous century, private police were hired to crackdown on the bootleggers. As fast as one hole was closed down, another would open and it got to the point where Pennsylvania State Police were called in to assist.

Due to the frenetic nature of these bootlegging operations, safety precautions were at a minimum. Poor tools, cheap powder, and inadequate attention to timbering resulted in many accidents with men being injured and even killed. For a short period, my father had a hole with several partners. They abandoned the project after a cave-in. Later, he was a helper on trucks transporting coal to Baltimore.

An article in the January 9, 1934 issue of the *Nation* estimated that 100,000 men, women, and children in Schuylkill and Northumberland counties were directly involved in bootlegging and accounted for the "theft" of four and a half to five million tons of coal from company lands in the previous 12 months.

But it should not be imagined that these miners were getting rich off the company. They were simply doing what they could to make a living for their families. It was hard and dangerous work. Few of those involved made more than $3 a day. My father said the usual practice when taking a load to a place like Baltimore was to go door to door, seeking buyers for the coal. Sometimes it took days or even weeks to sell the load. Meanwhile haulers had to eat, buy gas, and pay other expenses.

Though bootleg coal was seen as big business, the profits were spread thin among many people. It benefited not only individual miners and their families, it also kept stores, restaurants, banks, gas stations, and other businesses alive in the communities where it existed. An account in the *Reading Eagle* of December 2, 1934 estimated that 40 percent of all store sales in Pottsville came from bootleg mining money. For this reason, often the police and courts proved lenient when miners were arrested.

Because of these economic issues, George H. Earle III was sympathetic to the bootleggers when he took office as Pennsylvania's 30th governor in 1935. After a three-day rally in Harrisburg, which included some 200 truckers who were from the Shamokin area, Earle relaxed police pressure on bootleggers and even declared some county properties "free" to the miners.

A New Period

But pressure from the big operators made a crackdown inevitable. Newspapers across the nation carried a report from Harrisburg on October 15, 1943 that Pennsylvania was cracking down on the "... 12-year-old, depression-born economic fester" with a flat edict that all bootleg mining of hard coal must cease by November 30.

The order was issued by a committee established by the state legislature to control production and gradually eliminate the practice of unemployed miners trespassing on coal lands they did not own or lease.

"Trespassing on lands and stealing of coal will be outlawed in the anthracite region after Nov. 30, 1943," said a committee statement, "in the same manner that stealing is outlawed in any community. The active assistance of every law enforcement agency, both state and local, will be enlisted."

The reports said that 10 extensions had been granted by the committee after an original deadline of March 31, 1942 in response to miner pleas they had no other means of livelihood. The committee contended that further extensions were unnecessary because of growing opportunities for employment in legitimate occupations.

In response the Anthracite Tri-County Independent Miners, Breaker Men, and Truckers Association was actively lobbying in behalf of its membership. Their efforts resulted in the Independent Miners being placed under jurisdiction of the Pennsylvania Department of Mines in 1953. Enactment of the commonwealth law made independent miners subject to safety regulations and inspections to assure compliance. It also required payment of a royalty on coal mined from privately owned property and made them subject to state and federal taxes and environmental regulations.

The Future

There's still coal in the ground and mining continues in the region, though on a much smaller scale than in the past. With the exception of a few breakers here and there, most mining today is by independents, strip operators, and recovery efforts for co-generation plants like the Foster Wheeler facility near Mount Carmel.

The pristine wilderness pioneers found when the territory was first opened to settlement was destroyed in less than a century by the mining that provided wealth for the owners and employment for the thousands who came with their families and created thriving communities where there had been only mountains, forests, and swamps.

For the most part, they were moral, hardworking people who sincerely believed that man was meant to have dominion over the earth. Their labor sustained life here and contributed to the development of the nation.

While still important, coal no longer promises economic security for the region. For decades, community leaders have struggled to find a replacement for the industry.

Lack of "opportunity" is often blamed for the exodus of the best and brightest young people from the area. Yet, opportunity may lie at our doorsteps, ignored and unrecognized because it doesn't conform to preconceived notions of what it should look like.

Opportunity may exist in the form of culm banks, depleted stripping lands, and abandoned mines.

Some might say the only use for such wastelands is for landfills—and that has been tried in a few places with risky consequences.

I noted previously how culm was considered as a possible advantage way back in the 1890s. It is being harvested today for cogeneration. Could research reveal other uses? As a building product, a road-surfacing material, a battery filler? Could these mountains of waste conceal treasure?

Thomas Edison established a laboratory in Shamokin to be close to a source of carbon necessary to his electrical enterprises. Had he remained, perhaps his research could have left us another industrial legacy. Unfortunately, at the time, coal was the only industry we needed. Edison, and opportunity, was allowed to slip away to New Jersey where others were eager to provide funds for his experimentation.

Could our vacant lands be utilized for industrial parks, recycling facilities, campgrounds, even home sites and certain agricultural purposes? Is it unfeasible to consider using abandoned mines for mushroom production, archival storage, or warehousing?

Opportunity is a particular condition waiting to be molded to provide a means of profit. Work would be required to achieve the benefit.

Naturally, any of the proposals suggested would require investment of money, time and energy. The point is, there are alternatives other than landfills providing forward-looking people are willing to look for them.

BIBLIOGRAPHY

Bell, Herbert C., editor. *History of Northumberland County, Pennsylvania*, Chicago, 1891.

Bowen, Eli. *The Pictorial Sketch-Book of Pennsylvania and its Scenery, Internal Improvements, Resources and Agriculture*. Philadelphia, 1852.

Broehl, Wayne G., Jr. *The Molly Maguires*. Harvard University Press, Cambridge, MA, 1964.

De Crevecouer, J. Hector St. John. *Letters From an American Farmer*. Penguin, N.Y. 1981.

Franklin, Benjamin. *Observations Concerning the Increase of Mankind*. Philadelphia, 1751.

Godcharles, Frederic A. *Daily Stories of Pennsylvania*. Milton, PA., 1924.

Heckewelder, John. *History, Manners and Customs of the Indian Nations*. Heritage Books, 2009.

Johns, Dr. J. J. *Scrapbook No. 3*, collection of Northumberland County Historical Society, Sunbury PA.

Korson, George, editor. *Pennsylvania Songs and Legends*. University of Pennsylvania Press, 1949.

The majority of references are from contemporary newspapers. They include:

Ashland Record, Ashland, PA
Daily Item, Sunbury, PA
Dispatch, Shamokin, PA
Evening Item, Sunbury, PA
Evening News, Sunbury, PA
Gazette & Miner's Register, Sunbury, PA
Miners Journal, Pottsville, PA
New York Telegraph, New York City, NY
Northumberland County Democrat, Sunbury, PA
Philadelphia Inquirer, Philadelphia, PA
Public Ledger, Philadelphia, PA
Public Press, Northumberland, PA
Shamokin Citizen, Shamokin, PA
Shamokin Herald, Shamokin, PA
Shamokin Times, Shamokin, PA
Shamokin Weekly, Shamokin, PA
Shenandoah Herald, Shenandoah, PA
Sunbury American, Sunbury, PA
Tamaqua Courier, Tamaqua, PA
Workingmen's Advocate, Sunbury, PA

www.ingramcontent.com/pod-product-compliance
Lightning Source LLC
LaVergne TN
LVHW091218080426
835509LV00009B/1063